LIONEL PIGOT JOHNSON was born on March 15, 1867, at Broadstairs, and had a Celtic strain in his ancestry. He spent six years as a scholar in College at Winchester, and then proceeded to New College. He was a great admirer of Walter Pater, of whom he saw a good deal at Oxford. His literary period, so far as the public is concerned, may be said roughly to have extended from 1890 to 1900, when he lived in London and supported himself by various writing for periodicals, many of which have since been collected and published. The work for which he cared was always the unremunerative one of poetry. In 1891 he became a Roman Catholic, and he died at the age of thirty-five on October 4, 1902.[1]

RUTH DERHAM is a biographer and social historian whose work has centred on Victorian attitudes to marriage and divorce. Her first book, *Bertrand's Brother: The Marriages, Morals and Misdemeanours of Frank, 2nd Earl Russell*—a biography of the original editor and recipient of Lionel Johnson's Winchester Letters—was published in 2021; and her second, *Decadent Divorce: Scandal and Sensation in Victorian Britain*, is due for publication in 2024.

SARAH GREEN is a scholar specialising in the literature of the 1890s. Her monograph, *Sexual Continence and Aesthetic Experience in Victorian Literary Decadence*, was published by Cambridge University Press in 2023, and explored the work of Walter Pater, Lionel Johnson, Vernon Lee, and George Moore. She has also published on the work of J. M. Barrie and is particularly interested in the history of sexuality and sexual health. She lives in Cambridge, UK.

---

1 Biography written by Frank Russell in 1919, and taken from *Some Winchester Letters*.

THE COMPLETE WINCHESTER LETTERS
OF
LIONEL JOHNSON

EDITED BY
RUTH DERHAM AND SARAH GREEN

THIS IS A SNUGGLY BOOK

Copyright © 2024
by Ruth Derham and Sarah Green.
All rights reserved.

ISBN: 978-1-64525-140-8

CONTENTS

Introduction / 7
Editorial Note / 47
Sources / 49
Acknowledgments / 51

The Letters
    Part 1. In Search of a Creed / 55
    Part 2. I am a Priest! / 127
    Part 3. Brotherhood is God / 195

Appendix: Introductory material from
    Some Winchester Letters of Lionel Johnson / 275
Index / 281

INTRODUCTION

In the late summer of 1918 John Francis Stanley, 2nd Earl Russell—grandson and heir of former British Prime Minister Lord John Russell and elder brother of polymath Bertrand Russell—met with Cambridge librarian Charles Sayle, an old friend from his Oxford days. It must have been a curious meeting between men who last knew each other as 'Frank' and 'Charlie', as earnest, passionate, idealizing youths. They hadn't met since Russell left Oxford in his second undergraduate year, having been accused by the Master of his college, Benjamin Jowett, of 'disgusting conduct' that may have included the writing of a 'scandalous letter'.[1] Russell always strongly denied the charges, the full details of which remain unknown, though they dogged him throughout his highly litigious career. There is reason, as we will see, to think that Sayle was not ignorant of the true story.

The purpose of their meeting, after all this time, was to exchange the extraordinary letters written to them at Oxford by a mutual friend, the 1890s poet

---
1 Earl Russell, *My Life and Adventures* (London: Cassell & Co., 1923), 107.

and critic Lionel Johnson. Johnson had died suddenly of a brain haemorrhage in 1902, aged only 35, and Russell wanted to publish the correspondence—opportunity having recently provided the means. His secretarial work on behalf of his brother during Bertrand's incarceration in Holloway prison in 1918 for offences under the Defence of the Realm Act had brought Russell into contact with Stanley Unwin, who agreed that George Allen & Unwin would publish the correspondence as *Some Winchester Letters of Lionel Johnson* (1919). As a writer operating on the edge of the Decadent Movement, Johnson's too-short life had already been taken up by many memoirists as a symbol of what Yeats was to call the 'tragic generation'. Emphasis, exaggeration, and in some cases fantasy had been applied to his self-destructive habits and to the more theatrical elements of his life: his insomnia and alcoholism; his apparent retreat into literature and Catholic ritual; his close friendships with leading Decadent figures like Dowson, Douglas, and Pater; his unjustified claims to Irish heritage. In publishing Johnson's school letters, Russell at least partly intended to rescue his friend's legacy, to direct attention away from what he called 'such external facts about his life as have been forced upon my notice' and towards the Johnson he remembered (or wanted to remember): an intellectual and spiritual teacher intended 'for an angel of God', at whose feet the young Russell had sat 'as at the feet of Gamaliel'.[1]

---

[1] [Earl Russell], 'Introduction' in *Some Winchester Letters of Lionel Johnson* (London: George Allen & Unwin, 1919), 9-13, 11; *Life and Adventures*, 90.

The letters, he wrote in his anonymous 1919 introduction, 'deal not with personal and temporary affairs, but with general questions of a kind which have interested the whole thinking part of the human race for centuries'. And yet, alongside this universal appeal, Russell claimed that they showed the 'true Lionel', altogether more serious, spiritual, and elevated than the Decadent alcoholic insomniac of 1890s memoir.[1] In offering these letters to the world Russell wanted to pass on the lesson which he elsewhere said that he learnt from his friend: 'that all the supposedly real things of life, that is to say the external things, the physical things, the humours, the happenings, disgraces, successes, failures are in themselves the merest phantoms and illusions, and that the only realities are within one's own mind and spirit'.[2] By 1919 Russell himself, having passed through two painful and very public divorces, had much need of this wisdom; or at least believed the world, and particularly that part of the world that wrote for the newspapers, to be in need of it.[3]

To function as instructional resources, however, Johnson's letters required editing. This included removal of what was personal and contingent, such as names and many details that referred directly to their daily lives at Winchester College and Oxford: enquiries after friends, banal gossip, practical arrangements. It also involved excising sections in which Johnson

---

1 [Russell], 'Introduction', 9, 12.
2 Russell, *Life and Adventures*, 90-1.
3 For more about Russell's messy divorce, see Ruth Derham, *Bertrand's Brother: The Marriages, Morals and Misdemeanours of Frank, 2nd Earl Russell* (Stroud: Amberley Publishing, 2021).

responds to news of Russell's dramatic removal from Oxford, an event which eventually caused Johnson's father to ban all contact. If Russell had been hoping to turn attention away from biography, both Johnson's and his own, then he failed spectacularly. The anonymity of the edition—as well as omitting the editor's name, the letters were addressed simply to 'A', 'B' and 'C'—quickly inspired rumours that many long sections had been cut, the infamous nature of which was made more plausible by the threat of legal action from Johnson's remaining family if the book was not immediately withdrawn (it wasn't).[1] Until now the unknown location of many of these letters had prevented Russell's edition from being compared to the originals, and it has been taken for granted that what Murray Pittock has called 'extensive bowdlerization' took place to conceal… what? Proof of their writer's depraved character? References to drinking and other intoxicants? The sexual nature of the relationship between these affectionate and romantic young men?[2]

This edition restores for the first time the full text of the letters collected by Russell. Covering a period of nearly two years between October 1883 and July 1885, the letters are written by the 17/18-year-old Johnson at Winchester College to three slightly older friends at the

---

[1] *Ibid.*, 286.
[2] Murray Pittock, 'Introduction', in *Selected Letters: Lionel Johnson*, (ed.) Murray Pittock (Edinburgh: Tragona Press, 1988), 5-7; 6.

universities of Oxford and Cambridge: Frank Russell (A), Charles Sayle (B), and John Badley (C).

But who was Lionel Johnson, and what is there of interest today in his juvenile letters? Lionel Pigott Johnson was born in 1867 into a High-Church military family. He studied at Winchester College and New College, Oxford, before embarking on a literary career in London. He entered the Roman Catholic Church in 1891. Between 1890 and 1895 he lived in a room at the top of 20 Fitzroy Street, a house shared by literary and artistic men (including Arthur Mackmurdo, Herbert Horne, and Selwyn Image) at the centre of an artistic community wherein the Decadent Movement met Arts and Crafts. From there Johnson produced numberless literary reviews and articles and published two books of verse: *Poems* (1895) and *Ireland, With Other Poems* (1897). He also wrote *The Art of Thomas Hardy* (1894), the first book of criticism on that writer and unusual in treating of a living author. As a poet he was both formal and eclectic, showing the influence alternately of seventeenth-century metaphysical and religious lyric, eighteenth-century satire, and nineteenth-century Romanticism. Ezra Pound famously referred to his poems as 'small slabs of ivory', an example of what he saw as the 'hardness' produced by true scholarship rather than the 'softness' more typical of 1890s verse.[1] As a critic Johnson took it upon himself to defend what he called 'the broad and high tradi-

---

[1] Ezra Pound, 'Preface', in *Poetical Works of Lionel Johnson*, (ed.) Ezra Pound (London: Elkin Mathews, 1915), v-xix, ix; Ezra Pound, 'The Hard and the Soft in French Poetry', *Poetry*, 11:5 (February, 1918), 264-71, 267.

tions of literature'; a mission that for him most often involved, not castigation of what did not live up to his undeniably high standards, but rather praise of what did meet them wherever it could be found.[1] Thomas Hardy wrote to him that 'in your book you seem to be criticizing the stories as I imagined them before I had written them', and Michael Field wrote in their journal that he was 'the man who alone ever wrote words about our work that our souls countersigned'.[2]

In 1895, however, Johnson was asked to leave Fitzroy Street because his habits of lone nocturnal drinking were considered unsafe. He spent his remaining years moving between rooms in the Inns of Court and becoming increasingly involved in the Irish Literary Revival (although there was little basis to his claims of Irish heritage, it was not uncommon at this time to make the most of unpromising material). He lectured on Irish literature in Dublin in 1894 and 1898 and interested himself in Irish politics. He nevertheless became progressively isolated, as bouts of ill health (including crippling gout) and periods of drinking combined with the scattering and premature deaths of many of his literary friends after the Wilde trials of 1895 to cut off many lines of support. On 1

---

[1] Lionel Johnson, *The Art of Thomas Hardy* (London: John Lane, 1894), 4.

[2] Letter from Thomas Hardy to Lionel Johnson, October 26 1894, bound into a copy of *Ireland, With Other Poems*, Winchester College Archives, WICC194; [Katherine Bradley and Edith Cooper], *Works and Days: From the Journal of Michael Field*, (eds.) T & D. C. Sturge Moore (London: John Murray, 1933), 240.

October 1902 he suffered a series of brain haemorrhages and died after four days of unconsciousness. He was buried in St Mary's Catholic cemetery.

Such are the external facts of the life of Lionel Johnson. Around this core has accumulated a mass of conjecture, not always inaccurate in spirit but more than usually riddled with demonstrable factual error. It is not true, for instance, as W. B. Yeats claimed, that after Johnson's death an autopsy found 'that in him the man's brain was united to a body where the other organs were undeveloped, the body of a child'.[1] It was not true, either, as Thomas Wright wrote in his 1907 biography of Pater, that 'One night, in October, 1902, a policeman, performing his duty in Fleet Street, found a man lying unconscious on the pavement. It was Lionel Johnson. He died a few hours later in St. Bartholomew's Hospital'.[2] Ezra Pound recognised the symbolic potential of Johnson's life and death, as well as of the contest already emerging over his biography, in his poem 'Hugh Selwyn Moberly':

> [...] how Johnson (Lionel) died
> By falling from a high stool in a pub [...]
>
> But showed no trace of alcohol
> At the autopsy, privately performed—

---

[1] W. B. Yeats, *Memoirs*, (ed.) Denis Donoghue (London: Macmillan, 1972), 97. See Sarah Green, 'The Undeveloped Body of Lionel Johnson', *Notes and Queries*, 63:2 (June, 2016), 281-3.

[2] Thomas Wright, *The Life of Walter Pater* (London: Everett & Co., 1907), 221.

> Tissue preserved—the pure mind
> Arose toward Newman as the whiskey warmed.[1]

That the inquest suggested Johnson to have already suffered a stroke before he entered the pub, and that his autopsy was neither private nor commented on the presence of alcohol, is hardly the point. Pound identifies the coincidence between the insistence of some of Johnson's friends on his holy childlike innocence and the ever-increasing scepticism of others, as well as the convenient manner in which this dialectic encapsulated the early twentieth-century assessment of late Victorian literary culture as essentially hypocritical, consisting of a destructive combination of high-flown idealism and what T. S Eliot called 'untidy lives'.[2]

At the heart of the tussle over Johnson's legacy was his supposed retreat from the world, what Yeats called his having 'refused rather than failed to live'.[3] In practical terms this referred largely to his last few years, when Victor Plarr claimed to have been refused entry to his rooms (he calls this Johnson's 'mythic phase') and few acquaintances other than his laundress seem to have remembered seeing him recently.[4] But many memoirists used Johnson's supposed retreat from life

---

1 Ezra Pound, '"Siena Mi Fe": Disfecemi Maremma' (from the sequence 'Hugh Selwyn Moberly'), in *Collected Shorter Poems* (London: Faber & Faber, 1952), 210, lines 7-12.
2 T. S. Eliot, 'Arnold and Pater' in *Selected Essays,* 3rd ed. (London: Faber & Faber, 1951; essay first published 1932), 431-43, 442.
3 Yeats, *Memoirs*, 97.
4 Victor Plarr, *Ernest Dowson 1888-1897: Reminiscences, Unpublished Letters and Marginalia* (London: Elkin Mathews, 1914), 122.

as an interpretive tool to understand both his early death, and the tendency to 'tragedy' that seemed to plague his generation. His Catholicism, his fantasy of Irishness, his childlike appearance (he was often described as looking like a child of fifteen), his possible celibacy and/or homosexuality, even his insomnia and of course his alcoholism have been described as various methods of escaping the ordinary life of human beings. This symbolic approach to biography continued as literary memoir gave way to criticism, and retreat, refusal, and failure still form a crucial part of most readings of Johnson's life and work.

Nature abhors a vacuum. If the empty final years of Johnson's life act as an invitation to those with an agenda—arguably the case for those who portray him as a saint as much as those who find in him the arch-Decadent—this invitation has been immeasurably extended by the sheer lack of extant archival material with which a more accurate biography could be written.[1] In the 1940s and 50s a would-be biographer, Adrian Earle, gathered a mass of Johnson's manuscripts and letters, as well as those letters written to others and held in various private collections and archives (bestowed sometimes willingly, sometimes unknowingly). The biography was never written, and the material vanished. Very little has ever surfaced, but among the very few sales that Earle made was a bundle of letters addressed to Russell and Badley: the originals of those in *Some Winchester Letters*. The

---

1 The fullest biography to date is Richard Whittington-Egan, *Lionel Johnson: Victorian Dark Angel* (Malvern: Cappella Archive, 2012).

letters were purchased in 1949 by another would-be biographer, the Reverend Raymond Roseliep of Loras College in Iowa, who himself never completed the edition and biography that he contemplated. On his death in 1983 he donated the letters to his college archive, where they have lain undisturbed by Johnson scholars ever since.

Our intention in finally restoring the full text of these letters and those written to Charles Sayle (to be found in the University Library, Cambridge) is not to restore the 'true Lionel'. It is not our purpose to argue that Johnson was a good or bad Catholic, that he was or was not homosexual, or that he can or cannot be considered a Decadent. The content of the letters can be and has been used in support of any or all these arguments, and there is nothing in the restored sections to sway the vote decisively in one direction or another. Our primary intention is rather the opposite of any such argument. In restoring the personal and the contingent element that Russell excised, we hope to chip away at the retreat into myth and symbolism that has to some extent been forced onto both Johnson and late Victorian literary culture. Although an enormous body of excellent revisionary scholarship has recently been done on the period as a whole and especially on Aesthetic and Decadent literature, yet Johnson is most often mentioned (if he is mentioned at all) when older, less nuanced visions of the 1890s are invoked. In reversing Russell's editorial process, we want to dismantle his 'Epicurean god', but not to erect a Decadent idol in its place. We wish the restored letters to begin the difficult process of returning Johnson to his context.

The rest of this introduction will outline the events surrounding the writing of these letters, which can be constructed using the excised sections and Russell's journal entries from the period. The correspondence was not a series of wise pronouncements from a precocious prophet; it was strongly determined by the relationships between the writers, by their fluctuating intellectual infatuations and available reading material, and by the educational and domestic situations in which they found themselves. The letters are of great use to Johnson scholars by throwing light on the later development of his work, in exploring themes that would become dear to him. His assessment of different spiritual systems, for instance, can assist anyone attempting to understand why, as a reviewer, he praised certain writers and not others, and so shaped the literary taste of the 1890s. Further, his evident posturing, his testing out of ideas and modes of reasoning on a credulous audience, can provide a way out of biographical readings of his poetry, as that too can be read as experiments with different voices and intellectual or emotional postures. But the correspondence is often most entertaining when one perceives, not the mature and undeniably important writer that Johnson would become, but the 17-year-old that he was at that time. There is something delightful in the juxtaposition of high-flown Shelley-esque fantasy, such as the protest that 'I think you hardly realise the intense reality to some minds of the spirits: how they rustle their wings against our dusty, sin flushed, sorrow worn faces, and soothe them to sleep', with assurances that 'I go to gymnasium every day of my own accord, and am really developing somewhat, tho' yet no Hercules!'; something poignant in witnessing the absurdities of over-earnest youth in its groping towards self-knowledge and its attempts to understand or at least tolerate others.[1] If the correspondence is too contingent to give us the 'true Lionel', it nevertheless contains a version of truth that needs to be acknowledged; the truth of contingency itself.

A correspondence of which only one side survives will always be dissatisfying and intriguing in equal measure, and there are many points at which Johnson is obscure, either from intention or for want of the letters to which he was responding. There is often room for alternative interpretations of his meaning and motivations. While providing what we consider to be the most likely scenario we have tried to keep these alternatives open, and to indicate where major discrepancies could occur.

The letters begin a few days after Russell had gone up to Oxford for the first time, leaving Johnson behind at Winchester College. Johnson and Russell were unlikely friends. The structure of Winchester meant that they belonged to separate parts of the school with only rare opportunities for interaction. Johnson was a 'College man', belonging to the oldest and most academically driven section, while Russell was a 'Commoner', referring to a later expansion of the school for paying members of the upper classes. For the young Russell,

---

1 Letter 29.

whose ardent friendships were so often aspirational enthusiasms for qualities that he wished he possessed, this practical difficulty merely whetted his interest. Further fascination lay in their difference of character. Russell had been an unruly child, raised to be independent and free-thinking by aristocratic but unconventional parents. He suffered greatly when, on losing both parents by the age of 11, he found himself transferred to the stuffy mid-Victorian home of his elderly grandparents, Lord John Russell and his wife, Fanny, known as Lady John, who eventually sent him to Winchester in despair over his boisterous and occasionally violent behaviour. At school he responded surprisingly well to the combination of clear structure and the personal freedom that allowed the boys to roam the country (though not the city) in their leisure time. This physical liberty was accompanied by 'freedom to read any book we liked without censorship or supervision, and to write anything we liked'.[1] By the time he met Johnson his character was far more stable: he was full of intellectual enthusiasms though without an aptitude for schoolwork; morally and spiritually earnest to the point of priggishness; and thoroughly besotted with the school's atmosphere and traditions. But he was still easily riled to anger, especially by perceived injustice against himself, and his journal and autobiography record petty fights with his peers and absurd stands against authority over points of principle.

'I saw one day in my div. a small thin pale faced College man with an oval face and rather dark hair. It

---

1 Russell, *Life and Adventures*, 88.

was an arresting picture; he looked like some young saint in a stained-glass window.' Lionel Johnson at first appeared to Russell as 'aloof and detached' and 'apt to suggest an Epicurean god rather than a human being'. Ever enamoured of a challenge, Russell set to work to thaw this iciness and quickly found that Johnson 'didn't want to be like this, he passionately loved his fellow creatures in theory, but he found it very difficult in the flesh'. Johnson was by no means unsociable, but the constitutional shyness that appeared as cold aloofness meant that neither his editing of *The Wykehamist* (the school paper), nor his involvement with debating and Glee Club, nor his participation in the activities of the School Mission in Hampshire seemed to lead to many close friends. No doubt this supposedly inhumanely intellectual boy—he was rumoured, ridiculously, to have already in his first year read every book in the school library—greatly appreciated the characteristic purpose with which Russell pursued the unpromising friendship. They made good use of their few opportunities for meeting: in the library, walking in nearby countryside, and at cross-school tea parties. Russell later described Johnson as 'the greatest individual influence of my life at Winchester', though he 'was able to see more of him after I left the school than when I was in it'.[1] When Russell was suddenly removed from Winchester before his final term and sent first to a private tutor (much to his outrage), then to Oxford, they began a correspondence that

---

1 *Ibid.*, 89-90.

was to have a profound influence on both their lives.

On 4 October 1883 Russell wrote in his journal that on a visit to Winchester he had 'Met Johnson in Chamber Court about 12, and carried him off up Hills—we ran about on top, and down them and got blown by the glorious fresh wind, talked about Buddhism and other such like things and enjoyed ourselves quite immensely. [...] Reached Balliol about 6'.[1] The letters later identified by Russell as a series begin on 7 October, and the topic was again Buddhism. Russell had been introduced to Buddhism that summer by his older cousin St George Lane Fox-Pitt, an electrical engineer and inventor (later Liberal MP) with involvement in the Society for Psychical Research. Like many late Victorians St George was interested in Buddhism as a supposedly rational spiritual system that was in sync with the discoveries of science. Russell entered into the new faith with the passion with which he pursued everything he considered worth pursuing at all and couldn't wait to pass on the good news to his friend, though with a no doubt pleasant sense of mild naughtiness that prompted him to ask Johnson not to show the books he sent to anyone. To his horror Johnson was more cautious, responding, 'I quite feel the sense of power and nobility in the Buddhist system: but it revolts me'. Buddhism was, he complained, too elitist: 'religion', he wrote, 'must be popular, not scientific'.[2] 'Is it not rather hard

---

[1] Frank Russell Journals 1880-1890, William Ready Division, McMaster University, Ontario, *Bertrand Russell Archives*, RA1, box 731, 080042-080044; 080043, 36-7.
[2] Letter 2.

upon every day people', he continued, 'that they are placed, by no fault of their own, in situations in which this striving after the high state of spirituality would be impossible?'[1] There may have been awareness here of the difference in economic situation between the youngest son of a soldier (however genteel) and the soon-to-be Earl, as he refers to 'people who, like myself, must work to get their living'. This desire for spiritual equality led him instead to the pragmatic relativism to which he would resort when backed into a rational corner, much to the more intellectually black-and-white Russell's frustration. 'I have come more or less to the conclusion', Johnson wrote, 'that there is no absolute, universal Truth; that each of us has to struggle on, and make his Truth for himself'.[2]

But as Johnson read further into Buddhism his enthusiasm increased, while intellectually he found what he needed in the doctrine that 'ultimate perfection can be reached, even by those who cling to earthly ties, after a longer succession of trials and transmigrations'.[3] Nirvana was available to all, though some may take longer to get there than others. From then on, his commitment matches Russell's, and he is soon asking about his friend's attempts to spread the word at Oxford. Less than a month from his initiation he reports talking widely about Buddhism and introducing a defence into a school essay: 'I expect to be sat upon accordingly'.[4] This was trusting but unwise

---

1 Letter 3.
2 Letter 4.
3 *Ibid.*
4 Letter 7.

behaviour. Behind the boys' excitement the reader hears rumblings of alarm from their elders. On visiting Winchester in December 1883 Russell got 'a jaw' from Second Master George Richardson for 'proselytizing Johnson & wasting his time'. Shortly after he was summoned by his grandmother. He wrote in his journal that 'she pointed out to me the dangers of conceit & the need which I deeply feel of the spiritual and holy life as the very first step: I was seized with bitter remorse & deep penitence which I have not yet (Dec. 22) quite recovered from, & in my anguish I wrote a long letter to Johnson asking for comfort and encouragement'.[1]

Intervention did not stop there. Authorities in Winchester spoke to Johnson's father of their concern about the 'unhealthiness' of the correspondence, and the poor example to the school set by his son's shirking of chapel and other 'habits of solitude'. 'The Winchester people' Johnson reports, 'both pointed at my influence being pernicious, from a religious point of view, to the school, and suggested that if I did not get clear of the idea and habits of solitude, I should have to leave'.[2] Though this was no doubt a somewhat empty threat at this point, to understand the strength of the objection to 'habits of solitude' it is necessary to appreciate the importance of communal living at Winchester. The relative freedom of mind and body so valued by Russell was complemented, and to a certain extent made possible, by a complete absence of personal space. Russell records that, unlike other

---

1 Russell Journals, 080044, 132.
2 Letter 15.

schools such as Eton, at Winchester 'for no one at any time either by day or night was there any seclusion or privacy. There were no such things as cubicles, the beds in the Galleries were like a hospital ward; there were no such things as private studies, not even for the Prefects'.[1] The boys ate, slept, studied, worshipped, and played together. And although spending leisure time alone was not outlawed, school convention held that walks abroad would be taken with a companion. Johnson's letters had mentioned not only skipping the communal ritual of chapel (at least as important as the religious element and punishable with lines), but also going for long walks alone and at unusual times. Though by no means reluctant to take part in school life, Johnson's taste for solitude was evidently drawing attention in a world that equated seeking time alone with having something to hide. His pairing of the words 'solitary' and 'habit' refers ironically to the perennial single-sex boarding-school worry about masturbation: though the concern here is evidently not so specific, his phrasing shows awareness of the school's association of solitariness with unhealthiness, anti-social feeling, and moral perversity. Add to this the potential concern that Johnson, a well-behaved scholar whose opportunities in life depended on academic achievement, was being distracted and even corrupted by an errant child of the aristocracy, and it is easy to see why even the pragmatic and kindly (even Johnson concedes their 'good intentions') school authorities were worried enough to suggest parental sanctions.

---

1 Russell, *Life and Adventures*, 62.

The objections of Johnson's family, however, were of a different character: his father, he writes to Russell, 'views you as a clever individual, whose brain is full of corners, whose friendship is pernicious to me, as a Christian'.¹ Johnson was the youngest of four children and both parents were over 40 when he was born. The family were conservative and military—older brothers Ralph and Hugh both gained the rank of Captain, like their father—and both parents and sister Isabella were deeply religious High-Church Anglicans. As a male child unfitted for a military career by stature and temperament it is likely his parents hoped that he would enter the Anglican Church: if so, suspicion may have been rising that this future was in jeopardy. On arriving home and before suspecting the coming intervention, Johnson had written, 'I got here yesterday to find them all at Mass, and they are all at Church now. It is so strange to live in a world of intense faith!'² And although he professed to like this religious atmosphere, it had no doubt been noted that he had not joined them at Church. On publishing the letters in 1919 Russell wrote that Johnson had 'an arid home life', a judgement that even an early review said was unreasonable as the letters themselves did not 'eke out the malice', and which formed the basis of his sister Isabella's strong objection to the publication, along with distaste for the broadcasting of her brother's youthful religious doubts.³ The letters certainly show

---

1 Letter 15.
2 Letter 14.
3 [Russell], 'Introduction', 11; *Spectator* (10 January 1920), 19.

a lack of sympathy between father and son, but not necessarily a lack of affection or appreciation. When Captain Johnson responded to the school's concern by issuing a total ban on the correspondence, the edict was greeted by Johnson with sadness and resignation, by Russell with a fury and indignation that led him to describe his friend's parents in the 1919 edition as 'very narrow-minded and prejudiced Anglicans, to whom Buddha was apparently indistinguishable from anti-Christ'.[1] The letters, however, did not come to an end. Russell had been making new friends at Oxford, among them Charles Sayle. First described in his journal as 'about 5ft. high, of fat & ruddy countenance', Sayle was soon being recorded as 'the most loveable & warm hearted of men', with whom he could indulge in long talks on all matters 'personal & philosophic'.[2] Still smarting from the loss of Johnson, Russell showed his friend's letters to Sayle, an event that inspired a cunning work-around. Johnson would write not to Russell, but to Sayle, who would then reply on behalf of both, and in this manner the three young men could continue the spiritual and cultural discussions that had so engrossed the original two.

With this change the correspondence enters a new phase. Although Russell evidently did not consider Johnson's earlier letters to be strictly private productions they nevertheless read as if they are addressed to him personally, with recommendations of reading and explications of certain passages of poetry with which

---

1 [Russell], 'Introduction', 50.
2 Russell Journals, 080043, 94, 130.

he was struggling. As the correspondence opens to include Sayle ('B') and, later, a close friend of Sayle's at Cambridge, John Badley ('C'), a more public voice is adopted, and Johnson occasionally speaks as if expecting his letters to be read to a wider circle. The friends, and especially Russell, treated Johnson's subsequent letters as if they were in themselves religious texts to be puzzled over, interpreted, and (if possible) lived by. Russell's journal repeatedly refers to Johnson as 'infinitely above' them, and after breaking the ban to take Sayle to Winchester records that his new friend 'was struck with him just as I hoped & had acknowledged to me how high, exulted, pure & holy his noble spirit is: he tells me that he feels as I do, ready to fall down & worship him, & as if it was presumptuous to know him at all'.[1] Sayle's later diary contains an undated list of short excerpts from letters addressed to all three men, as if they were inspirational aphorisms or favourite biblical quotations.[2]

At the same time, however, the somewhat paternal tone of Johnson's earlier letters to Russell (in fact the elder of the two) quickly gives way to a self-conscious posturing and performativity that one can only assume to be in response to Sayle's own intellectual pretentions. Increasingly the letters push an intellectual position or posture to extremes, only to retreat again when the expressions of distress in return became too earnest. Sayle's secular humanism, for instance,

---

1 *Ibid*, 080044, 163.
2 Charles Sayle Diaries vol. 1 1864-1896, University Library, Cambridge, *Charles Sayle Diaries and Papers*, MS Add.8501, paper pasted between 270-1.

prompts him to a heightened spiritual idealism that is by turns intellectually engrossing and delightfully absurd, as when he claims to have 'often gone into church yards and even, when possible, vaults and charnel houses, to try to hear the truth from the lips of spirits, to force the paraphernalia of death to unfold their secret' (there is barely suppressed irritation in the start of the following letter: 'I *do* know Shelley').[1] This is the Johnson who would later take pleasure in testing the credibility of new acquaintances: whom George Santayana remembers boasting that 'when of age he intended to become a Catholic' (he did) 'and a monk' (he didn't) but 'at present his people, who were Welsh' (they weren't) 'objected'; and who boasted to W. B. Yeats of his (erroneous) personal friendships with Newman and Gladstone.[2] While these letters undoubtedly represent Johnson's first working out of many theories and principles that would later become important to his mature work—for instance, his preference of intuition over reason and desire to transcend ego (he was not unaware of the potential contradiction here)—it is important not to lose sight of their writer as a youth who is sometimes irked by intellectual competition and sometimes thoroughly enjoying his ability to make an impression.

---

1 Letters 18 and 19.
2 George Santayana, *Persons & Places*, critical edition, (eds.) W. G. Holzberger & H. J. Saatkamp (Cambridge, MA: MIT Press, 1986), W. B. Yeats, *Collected Works,* (general eds.) Richard J. Finneran and George Mills Harper, 14 vols. (New York: Scribner, 1984-ongoing), vol. 3: *Autobiographies*, (eds.) William H. O'Donnell and Douglas N. Archibald (1999; this section first published 1922), 237.

As the correspondence progressed a more serious question arose: if Johnson eschewed both rationalism and dogmatism entirely, did he deny moral laws? Before he could formulate his theories, however, the issue took an uncomfortably practical turn. Russell received at Oxford rumours of 'immoral behaviour' on Johnson's part supposedly precipitating calls for him to leave Winchester (though these 'calls' evidently did not this time involve the Winchester authorities or Johnson's family). It is difficult to reconstruct exactly what these 'terrible charges' involved. Russell invited a mutual friend, William Orange, to tea 'to extract the world's view' and was told that it was 'as bad as could be' and 'known to the world'.[1] Johnson's response to his friends' questions suggests that sensuality was involved, and that the main issue as far as he was concerned was his toleration of supposed sin in others rather than sins committed himself (no doubt rumour went beyond this). 'I will give you the best account of myself that I can', he wrote; 'I will begin with two statements: I am a Browningite: I love the beautiful Quaker doctrine, "Love the sinner and condemn (hardly that: depends on case) the sin"'. The letter that follows is a defence of tolerance, of living according to one's lights and allowing others to do so also, but couched in a defensive, immature aestheticism: 'I do not love sensuality: I do not hate it: I do not love purity: I do not hate it: I regard both as artistic aspects of life'. As a school prefect, however, he was responsible for regulating and disciplining the behaviour of his peers, and it appeared that this shirking of

---

1 Russell Journals, 080044, 163-4.

responsibility was at the heart of the accusations. 'As a prefect', he asserted, 'I will not take steps in the matter of "immorality": as a junior I never shrunk back from any society: I do not *now*'.[1]

Russell was heartbroken. He confided to his journal 'My basis of morality totters… I cannot understand, is it my blindness? Or am I right in my moral code? I should say so unhesitatingly to anyone else, but when one so infinitely above me as J… says thus, I hardly dare resist'. Sayle, on the other hand, seemed to object far less than Johnson anticipated.[2] Does Sayle's appreciation of a position that Johnson thought he would consider 'sham' provide a clue as to the 'immorality' that Johnson had tolerated in those under his authority as prefect? Sayle later claimed to have 'woke up' to his 'true nature' while at Rugby School, and later kept a diary full of details of his romantic, sensual attractions to other boys and men.[3] He responded to Johnson's defence by sending a bundle of anonymous poetry, very probably his own drafts of what would become *Bertha: A Story of Love* (1885), a collection of idealizing verse about male love. If he expected sympathy for his sentiments, he must have been disappointed. Johnson returned the manuscript rather coldly 'without having really had time to study it' and decreed that the author had 'absorbed too much Shelley to be good for his poetry'.[4]

More moral distress was to come. Barely a week after having refused to acknowledge universal moral truth

---

1 Letter 23.
2 Russell Journals, 080044, 163.
3 Sayle Diaries, 24 November 1893, 19.
4 Letter 24.

('how can I? am I eternal?'), Johnson declared his resolution to become a priest in the Church of England.[1] The decision was practical rather than based in divine conviction: 'I do long with all my energies of hope to be an influence'.[2] His broad, emotive spiritualism would be of more comfort to the poor and the needy, he argued, than Sayle's secular humanism, regardless of factual truth. But this spiritual pragmatism was too much for Russell, who after another illegal visit to Johnson at Winchester to remonstrate in person began again to lobby his grandmother to intervene to lift the ban on correspondence. This time he was successful, and he wrote effusively to Captain Johnson that 'I was not as wicked as I was painted'. The reply hoped that 'I may now depend upon you both and trust I may never have reason to regret the confidence I place in you'.[3] And yet the ban perhaps had something of its intended effect and had at least temporarily defused the ardour on Johnson's side at least. The transition back to individual letters was evidently not a smooth one, and one feels Johnson struggling to balance the intense but somewhat impersonal emotiveness of his intellectual discourses with a more detached real-life bonhomie.

The coherence of the correspondence was saved by a new enthusiasm: Walt Whitman. Although Johnson had read and admired Whitman already, Russell's discovery of the poet allows him to find common ground

---

1 Letter 25.
2 Letter 26.
3 Russell Journals, 080044, 180; Captain Johnson's reply was printed in *Some Winchester Letters*, 124.

in the now different (though perhaps not entirely separate) conversations that he was having with his two friends. Russell was still hung up on the problem of Johnson's excessive moral toleration, while Sayle objected primarily to the apparent metaphysical hypocrisy of his intention to become a priest. Both charges could be answered, even if exacerbated, through a Whitmanesque preaching of universal Brotherhood and pragmatism. To Russell: 'Whitman takes this world and shews that nothing is common or unclean: not even uncleanliness'.[1] To Sayle: 'Whitman would let me seek ordination at the hands of a bishop or else abjure his own principles: am in inconsistent? very well then, I am inconsistent'.[2] This approach to truth infuriated Sayle in particular, and emotions ran high. 'You intend cruelty', Johnson remonstrates in reaction to a letter accusing him openly of insincerity and lies.[3]

The new term brought new responsibilities for Johnson as senior prefect, Prefect of Chapel, member of the Mission Committee, and editor of the school magazine. It also saw a renewal of correspondence with John Badley, a close friend of Sayle's with whom he had established the Rugby school magazine *The Leaflet*. Johnson and Badley had corresponded earlier in connection to *The Leaflet*, to which Johnson had contributed a few lyrics, and it may have been this earlier connection that Russell intended to indicate when he misdated one of the letters so that it appeared much earlier in his collection. The new blood was cer-

---

1 Letter 42.
2 Letter 44.
3 Letter 47.

tainly needed to defuse tensions, and it was some time before the letters to Badley reach the effusion of those to Russell and Sayle.

Various visits over the next few months infused the correspondence with the much-needed fresh air of the practical world. Russell visited Johnson at the family home in Rhual, Wales, and Johnson returned the visit at Pembroke Lodge. Russell evidently made an effort and something of a good impression with the Johnsons, and Johnson wrote to Sayle that Russell 'reproaches me with intentional cruelty towards my people—a strange side of the matter'. But Sayle's spirit of controversy was evidently grating on Johnson, who wrote 'religion is the ideal platitude in personal intercourse: and it sickens me inexpressibly', ending the letter, 'I won't continue: I feel angry and rude'.[1] 'Why is Charley in a state of meaningless wrath and sorrow against me?' he complains to Badley, and months pass with few letters between the two.[2]

On 18 April 1885, however, Johnson finally visited Oxford and revelled not only in the presence of Russell and Sayle, but also in the wider atmosphere of freedom and comradery. He was taken to the Dolores, an eccentric club for the reading of obscure verse, and generally rejoiced in 'the personal delight and fascination of contact with free life and free love'.[3] At various points in these letters, Johnson refers to a difficulty with social interaction that seems to go beyond shyness, and which prompted Russell later to assert

---

1 Letter 66.
2 Letter 68.
3 Letter 79.

that 'friendship with Lionel Johnson in any ordinary personal sense was not a very easy thing'.[1] At Oxford he appears to have found the ground already prepared for him, and he wrote effusively to Sayle: 'You were very good to me at Oxford: and marvellously refused to be frozen and chilled by the iciness of my calm self-sufficing—for which I thank you'.[2] To Russell he admits 'as you know by experience, I have never been externally emotional nor receptive—I slip away into cold conceit or dull passivity. [...] I know by the personal standard of my impressions that I have been unusually happy with you—I gave you no reason for thinking so: but ça va'.[3]

But despite this renewed harmony it isn't long before he manages again to outrage Russell's, and possibly even Sayle's, moral sense, and is required to take a defensive attitude once more. Referring to a new acquaintance made at Oxford, he writes to Russell that 'Henn foolishly insisted upon carrying away some of my sins of commission in the way of verse: the quasi-dramatic sketch is uninteresting except to me as an experiment in form and metre and music: but I also gave him a few lyrics I wrote a few days before coming to you: will you see what you can make of them?' He continues, 'perhaps I may confess that most of them are addressed to a man here in Junior Part, a commoner, whom I have scarcely spoken to: but whom I cannot forget'.[4] This sentence is missing from *Some Winchester*

---

[1] Russell, *My Life and Adventures*, 89.
[2] Letter 80.
[3] Letter 81.
[4] *Ibid.*

Letters. The verses in question are very likely those sent by Henn later in life to the Johnson critic Ian Fletcher, and reproduced by him in his edition of Johnson's poems as 'Poems from the Henn MS'.[1] These love lyrics, uniquely in Johnson's surviving oeuvre, are openly addressed to a male subject and make repeated reference to both Johnson's family home in Wales and to Winchester as the place of encounter with the beloved. One poem, numbered '2' by Fletcher and possibly the 'quasi-dramatic sketch' referred to by Johnson, dramatizes thinking about the beloved during the Easter Church services, and uses this plainly sexual feeling to consider the relationship between religious and worldly passion: 'For I am passion-struck: ah from this thin / wan radiance of Friday smiles that sin / It were so fair to win; / So fair to die within?'[2]

Even with the possible disowning of this more explicit and personal portrayal as a mere 'experiment in form and metre', Johnson cannot have thought that Russell would take the verses lightly. The late nineteenth-century line between romantic friendship and homosexuality was at once the strongest and most fragile of lines, especially in single-sex environments such as public schools and universities, and much agony was expended on the differences (or similarities) between spiritualized affection, sensuous appreciation of beauty, erotic but physically unexpressed love, and sensual indulgence. Johnson's flippancy suggests an

---

1 Ian Fletcher (ed.), *The Collected Poems of Lionel Johnson*, 2nd ed. (New York & London: Garland Publishing, 1982), 246-54.
2 *Ibid.*, '2', 247, lines 36-9.

awareness that, in openly suggesting that his feeling towards another boy was erotic as well as affectionate, he was transgressing what to Russell was an unnegotiable boundary. The resulting moral agony was not quite as strong as it had been a year earlier, when the question was almost certainly of Johnson tolerating actual sexual actions on the part of others. But it is hardly surprising to find Russell accusing Johnson of, in Johnson's own words, having 'changed from a lofty pedestal of aspiration to the vulgar level of cowardly acquiescence'. 'You think less of me?' he summarizes; 'I may still pose as a friend perhaps, but no longer as a priest of the Most High? You will write to me when you want to waste a few minutes in light and casual converse, but will keep a reproachful silence when you are spiritually inclined for sympathy?' The problem for Russell was evidently not, however, simply the homoerotic nature of Johnson's romantic sentiments, but extended rather to what he saw as his irreverence for truth. 'So you don't know when to believe me: well, is not that sense of uncertainty an element of strength to yourself?'[1]

Just as the correspondence seemed about to fall back into a familiar pattern, however, the tables took a dramatic turn. By far the largest sections cut from the Russell's original publication of *Some Winchester Letters* were from the final ten letters. In the same letter in which Johnson replies to Russell's claim to now think less of him, he returns to him a correspondence with 'the Master', Benjamin Jowett of Balliol (Russell's college at Oxford). 'You tell him plainly that

---
1 Letter 82.

he is talking wild nonsense at random', he says.[1] So began an episode that was to have a profound effect on Russell's life and give his friends a nasty shock. In his *My Life and Adventures* (1923) Russell tells how he was called unexpectedly into Jowett's rooms and told 'he had been informed that I had been guilty of disgusting conduct in writing some scandalous letter'. At this point, in Russell's account, Jowett was willing to believe that the letter was 'only a piece of thoughtlessness' and suggested sending him away from Oxford for a month as punishment. But the accusation, together with Jowett's inability to be more precise about what the letter contained and refusal to inquire, enraged Russell:

> I was startled beyond belief by such an accusation, and I was also infuriated by his calm way of talking to me as if it could possibly be true. So remote was it from the truth that I was entirely possessed by that white virginal flame of innocence which I think is even stronger in adolescent boys than in girls, and I was horrified that it should be possible for anyone in close relation with me to think otherwise.

The situation quickly escalated, with Jowett offering ever harsher punishments and Russell telling him 'that he was no gentleman, that he was behaving in an autocratic way, indefensible even in the head of an

---

1 *Ibid.*

Oxford college, and that I refused to have anything more to do with him'. Eventually 'I left Oxford in May, 1885, accompanied to the railway station and seen off by scores of enthusiastic friends and defiantly wearing in my buttonhole the white flower of a blameless life'. Forgiveness was a long time coming. 'My soul was filled with wrath and hatred and for at least six months afterwards I used solemnly to put on my cap and gown every Sunday and sit in the garden and curse Jowett.'[1]

The incident had an undeniable impact on Russell's life and career. Aside from yet again being exiled from the community of equals that he so sorely craved, the charge of homosexual behaviour was used as a weapon of defamation in Russell's very public encounters with the law: his two appearances in the divorce court with first wife Mable Edith Scott and his subsequent prosecution of his mother-in-law, Lady Selina Scott, for criminal libel at the Old Bailey. Although far from sexually reticent, Russell always strongly denied sexual attraction to men, and his simple, self-righteous account of the Oxford incident is both in keeping with and the foundation for this denial. And yet George Santayana, who knew Russell well in the period following his leaving Oxford, recorded a very different account of the matter. Russell's story was, he said, 'a cheeky lie, when so many of his readers know the facts' and 'a complete falsification of the events as told me by Russell himself'.[2] According to Santayana, the

---

1 Russell, *Life and Adventures*, 107-8.
2 Written by Santayana in the margins of his copy of Russell's *My Life and Adventures*, later published in John McCormick

Oxford authorities had objected not just to a mysterious letter, but also to rumours that Russell had had in his rooms an overnight visitor who was too young to be his 'natural friend'. This was, Santayana claimed, none other than the notoriously youthful-looking Johnson on his 18 April Oxford visit. And although the relation between Russell and Johnson was not, he asserted, 'in the least erotic or even playful', yet there were 'early obscenities' in Russell's history that made the charges somewhat less 'remote from the truth' than he claimed. It is unclear whether these 'obscenities' were explicitly confided to Santayana by Russell himself or extrapolated, rightly or wrongly, from experience of his friend's character.[1]

Johnson's letters do not provide a full account of the Oxford incident, nor do they give any decisive evidence regarding 'obscenities'. But they do support Santayana in suggesting a much more protracted, painful, and complex affair than that related by Russell. As with the Buddhism episode, Johnson does not at first grasp the seriousness with which the news would be treated by his elders. He expresses his 'real satisfaction at late occurrences', congratulating his friend for having finally achieved a freedom that would allow him to live his life as he deemed fit. The charges themselves he treats as unfathomably petty, professing not to understand the jurisdiction which

---

(ed.), *George Santayana's Marginalia: A Critical Selection*, 2 vols. (Cambridge, MA: MIT Press, 2011), vol. 2, 217-18.

1 The story appears in the 1986 critical edition of Santayana's *Persons and Places*, 309. It was not included in previous editions, but rather was recorded by Santayana in private notebooks.

the authorities at Oxford seemed to claim over what he saw as a matter of private conscience. 'As an outsider', he writes, 'I am unable to understand the incredible fatuity of Oxford dignitaries—what do they mean by immorality? [...] how can the Warden of Merton and Spooner, etc, actively concern themselves in the matter of your morality?' This is still several months before the Labouchere Amendment to the Criminal Law Amendment Act 1885 would make not only acts of 'gross indecency' between men 'in public or private', but also 'attempts to procure the commission' of such acts, a crime punishable with imprisonment and hard labour. This amendment would elevate Russell's letter, if it existed, from a matter of personal conscience to potential evidence of criminal acts possibly committed or the attempt to incite such acts. And though it is unlikely that those involved in Russell's dismissal from Oxford would have anticipated this dramatic but very last-minute change in law, yet the spirit of public interest in private morals by which it was motivated appeared to be further advanced, unsurprisingly, with those in charge of young lives than with the young men themselves. Johnson appears both genuinely puzzled, and yet aware that the situation could deteriorate, writing to Russell that 'beyond all the little trivialities and mean follies of all this matter, I recognise the high laws of freedom at stake'.[1]

But what had Russell done, if anything? At first Johnson evidently does not have the full details and asks, 'do they mean to pin definite acts upon you, or merely cast your general ideas and manner of life

---
1 Letter 84.

against you?' He does not, however, assume his friend's entire innocence in the way Russell later claimed to expect from Jowett. 'Let me know the precise charge, if there is one: if they can point to actual facts capable of offending their vulturine nostrils, I see no other course than to accept their judgment: if they are merely vague and vindictive and venomous, face them with Walt and Jesus—defend your soul and body—either way you will be perfectly tranquil.' Johnson appears inclined to consider that the question is not, as it was over his poems, whether a romantic same-sex affection involved sensual feeling or not (Whitman and Jesus could be taken to stand for sensual and non-sensual versions of same-sex affection respectively), but whether that sensuality had been manifested in sexual acts. In his enthusiasm he groups himself and Russell together as denying that 'love must be eschewed when it claims domination and lordship upon the flesh', before realising that this is not consistent with Russell's objections against his own behaviour: 'You have lately reproached me with my self-assertion, assumption of omniscience, and spoken of your own conscience, your ideas of right and wrong: there would seem to be a difference somewhere'.[1] And yet he still feels the need to ask, 'understand me: have you technically incurred legal penalties? don't be angry: you don't suspect me'.[2]

There are indications that Johnson at least suspected the issues at stake. 'Has my name turned up again?' he asks, implying that Santayana's story was not unfounded. But it seems unlikely that, at this point, his

---
1 *Ibid.*
2 Letter 85.

visit is the main concern. From the beginning, Johnson presumes that whatever has happened concerns not only Russell, but Sayle also. 'I don't know what either you or Charlie mean to do in life', he says, 'and this business may have serious results in that direction'.[1] Sayle's involvement would certainly account for the interest of Reverend Spooner, Dean of New College, where Sayle was an undergraduate; though it is possible that Spooner would also have taken an interest in a case involving a promising Winchester student, New College having a close relationship with that school. A contemporary, however, later remembered of Russell and Sayle that 'they behaved sentimentally, even in public; at a concert R[ussell] & S[ayle] sate hand in hand'.[2] On 30 May Johnson refers to having written to Sayle and had a reply, though the last letter in this series was over a month previous. Was that letter not kept like the others? And as matters deteriorated and more and more friends withdrew support, Johnson asks Russell 'At the risk of seeming obtrusive, let me ask you whether you still think [Charlie] worthy of your sacrifice?'[3] Was Russell unable to 'speak out' as regards the facts of the case because doing so would incriminate Sayle? Or was he unable in good faith, or indeed unwilling, to publicly deny the sentiments that had raised suspicion?

The situation escalated swiftly and brutally. In June there was talk of a summer of visits to and fro:

1 Letter 84.
2 Recollections of Henry Newbolt, Magdalene College, Cambridge, *Diaries of Arthur Christopher Benson*, vol. 175, ff. 39-40.
3 Letter 92.

Russell to Johnson in Winchester, Johnson to Sayle and Badley in Cambridge (where Sayle's family lived), Badley to Russell. By July, Badley becomes uncertain that he will be allowed to visit Russell, and then suddenly Johnson writes to Badley, 'I cannot go to Charlie's [...] Neither can I go to Russell's. I have no time for further explanations.' He ends the letter, 'We shall never meet—but I could not love you better than I do, dear brother'.[1] Evidently suspicion had spread beyond Russell. His penultimate letter to Russell reveals that Russell was no longer welcome at Winchester, at least for the time being. Even worse, Johnson's father had written to Jowett to enquiry about the reasons for Russell's leaving Oxford and had been told that he was 'a very improper friend', and recommended to 'forbid any further acquaintance between his son and Lord Russell'.[2] He did just that. 'My father is impenetrable', Johnson moans; 'professes real affection for you, but resolutely declines to sanction correspondence—on pains of rejection and expulsion and disinheriting, etc—whilst he has told the Winchester people to stop letters passing'. His frustration and grief are evident, though it is characteristic that his blame is always directed to the abstract force of convention—'how it enslaves and encircles and paralyzes' - rather than at individuals. 'So, until I am legally master of myself, I must say goodbye—they know not what they do.'[3] And so, the correspondence abruptly ends.

---
1 Letter 91.
2 Letter from Benjamin Jowett to John Ffolliott, 5 July 1885, Balliol College, Oxford, *Jowett Papers*, IV/A8/24.
3 Letter 93.

※

Russell took his wounded heart and pride to a semi-detached house on the north bank of the Thames, which he named Ferishtah after Browning's recent collection *Ferishtah's Fancies* (1884). His friendship with Johnson would recover though life took them in very different directions, and his letters were always treasured as repositories of wisdom. Sayle, however, Russell did not see again until 1918. Shortly after Russell's exile from Oxford, Sayle finally published *Bertha: A Story of Love* (1885) and was accordingly rusticated for the remainder of the academic year. In 1893 he became librarian at Cambridge University Library, where he remained for the rest of his life. Johnson joined Sayle at New College in 1886, where their friendship remained close but less intense as his circle of connections widened and audience expanded. Badley became interested in education, and in 1893 co-founded Bedales School, the first coeducation public boarding school in England. His 1955 memoir *Memories and Reflections* mentions Johnson as a 'true poet' with whom he corresponded 'until in my case absorption in educational work took the place of earlier dreams'.[1] Sayle is even more briefly remembered as a friend with whom he co-founded *The Leaflet*, and Russell (who had died in 1931) is not named at all.

The letters that follow constitute an important stage in the intellectual, emotional, and spiritual de-

---

[1] J. H. Badley, *Memories and Reflections* (London: George Allen & Unwin, 1955), 62.

velopment of a figure who would go on to become a major shaping force in the cultural life of 1890s London. They also show three young men struggling to assimilate their own feelings and enthusiasms to the seismic shifts that were taking place in religious feeling, in conceptions of sexuality, and in the ever-narrowing divide between public and private spheres. But perhaps most of all, they offer an endearingly humane portrait of a person so often considered too 'aloof and detached' to really be of relevance to either his own time or to ours. We hope that readers will join us in refusing to be 'frozen and chilled' by Lionel Johnson, and instead approach his writing in the spirit of generosity and warmth that to him was always the mark of true culture and true love.

EDTORIAL NOTE

The letters produced here were identified as a series by Earl Russell in his *Some Winchester Letters of Lionel Johnson* (1919). They have been re-transcribed from the originals, with sections excised from Russell's edition restored. The originals of those addressed to Russell and John Badley are held at Loras College (Dubuque, Iowa), while the originals of those addressed to Charles Sayle and those of Letters 77 and 84 (addressed to Russell) are held at the University Library at the University of Cambridge (Cambridge, UK). We have supplemented this series with one letter (63) addressed to Russell, held at McMaster University (Hamilton, Ontario), which contains relevant information concerning Russell's visit to Johnson in Wales in January 1885.

In transcribing the letters we have remained as close to the originals as is consistent with the production of a clean and readable text. Johnson's idiosyncratic style of punctuation and spelling (i.e. Bhuddism) have been retained, as has inconsistencies of spelling (i.e. 'apologise' and 'apologize') and shortening of words ('shld', 'wld', 'Xtianity') the expansion of which may have altered tone. We have, however, occasionally supplied missing apostrophes and speech marks, and silently corrected the very small number of evident misspellings. Where missing words have been supplied, they have been given in square brackets. Johnson rarely deleted text, and we have omitted minor deletions except where they contained potentially significant information. We have used italics for titles and to indicate where Johnson underlines text.

Address and date formats have been standardized and justified to the right, and square brackets used to indicate information added by anyone other than Johnson. Occasionally we have silently supplied location based on the headed paper on which the letter is written. Russell habitually dated letters on receipt, and we have accepted this testimony. Letters to Badley are dated in an unknown hand, possibly Badley himself, and these dates have been retained where they are not contradicted by the text. Those to Charles Sayle, however, are often undated, and several were ascribed erroneous dates by Russell during editing. We have noted where letters have been re-dated or re-sequenced and have given our reasons for doing so. Johnson occasionally continued his letter at the top or side of previous pages; we have uniformly moved these afterthoughts to the end.

Notes have been added to provide essential historical and contextual information; to identify quotations where possible and where the provenance is not obvious; to identify persons or works that may not be readily recognizable by a general reader; and to translate non-English phrases and quotation.

SOURCES

Archival Material

<u>Cambridge University</u>
Charles Sayle Diaries and Papers, University Library, MS Add.8501-8513.
Diaries of Arthur Christopher Benson, Magdalene College, Pepys Library, vol. 175.

<u>Loras College, Dubuque, Iowa</u>
Winchester Letters, Roseliep Personal Papers, Filing Cabinet A, Drawer 1, Folders 3-7.

<u>McMaster University, Ontario</u>
Frank Russell Journals 1880-1890, William Ready Division, Bertrand Russell Archives, RA1, box 731, 080042-080044.
Letter from Johnson to Russell, 26 Dec 1884, RA1, box 628, 080061.

<u>Oxford University</u>
Jowett Papers, Balliol College Archives, IV/A8/24.

Rugby School Archives
The Leaflet

Winchester College Archives
Copy of *Ireland, With Other Poems* bound with letters by Johnson, WICC194.
Daybook of Caldwell Harper, vol.3, 12 Apr 1883-11 Jun 1884, G12/3.
The Wykehamist

Reference Works
Anonymous, *Crockford's Clerical Directory for 1885*, 17th ed. (London: Horace Cox, 1885).
Foster, Joseph, *Oxford Men* (Oxford: James Parker, 1893).
Stevens, Charles, *Winchester Notions* (London: Althone press, 1998).
Wainwright, John Bannerman, *Winchester College, 1836-1906: A Register* (Winchester: P&G Wells, 1907).

ACKNOWLEDGEMENTS

We are grateful to Joyce Meldrum, Heidi Pettitt and the staff at Loras College archives for guiding us through the Raymond Roseliep Papers and to the staff at University Library Cambridge for their assistance with the papers of Charles Sayle. Suzanne Foster, archivist at Winchester College, made herself available to answer all manner of questions concerning life at the school and we are appreciative of her knowlcdge and enthusiasm and thankful for her help and support throughout the editing of these letters. Our gratitude also to Alex Wong for Greek and Latin translations; to Jean-Michel Johnston and William Bruneau for translating French and German phrases; to Anna Fonti of Snuggly Books for bringing this project to fruition; and to the Warden and scholars of Winchester College for permission to reproduce the photograph of Lionel Johnson used on the cover of this volume. Finally, we would like to acknowledge Frank, Earl Russell, for bringing together the original 'Winchester Letters' and Raymond Roseliep, for his preliminary work on the Russell and Badley letters and for bequeathing to Loras College a collection that would otherwise have remained obscure.

THE COMPLETE WINCHESTER LETTERS
OF
LIONEL JOHNSON

PART 1
IN SEARCH OF A CREED

1

College[1]
October 7, [1883]

Dear Russell,[2]

The same post that brought me your welcome letter, brought me another from a clerical friend of mine; a young man of ultra High Church views; amongst other amusing remarks, he said that, as my spiritual welfare was his especial care, he would 'warn me against the latest development of infidelity: the devil would come to me, robed even as an angel of light, and would seduce even the very elect; he referred to a strange movement in connection with Buddhism, which was so fascinating in its assumption of high spiritual tone, that he was certain it would ensnare me

---

1 The buildings within Winchester College that house the scholars or 'College men'.
2 John Francis Stanley Russell, 2nd Earl Russell (1865-1931), known to friends as Frank. Russell had met Johnson at Winchester College, and had recently moved to Balliol College, Oxford. He published an edited, anonymous version of these letters as *Some Winchester Letters of Lionel Johnson* (1919).

to my perdition.' I am meditating a fitting reply to this excellent young man. I saw Wells[1] yesterday, and he told me he would send up to College some pamphlets &c. which you had mentioned to him. I congratulate you on passing smalls,[2] though it is somewhat of an insult to do so. I also congratulate you on your first plunge into the turbid waters of Browning. The subject for next Thursday's debate is the Restoration of the Monarchy in France; the vivisection question, if accepted as a subject, would come on next Thursday fortnight. I have not the smallest wish to go into the Church; but my choice of a career is limited to that and literature; to tell you the truth, I should like to burst upon the astonished world as a poet; there you have the height of my ambition. Somewhat conceited, is it not? but the amount of poetry, if I may use the word, that I have already perpetrated, would fill a respectable volume. I should like to turn out a kind of Matthew Arnold in a more professedly 'religious' way; i.e., combine the position of a man of letters with that of a quasi-religious lecturer. The only reason I should have for taking orders would be the intense desire of getting hold of some of the rotten old pulpits occupied by dotards, and exploding some more sensible and higher doctrines than any I have yet heard; but the explosion might bring the Church down about my ears. People of a certain class might accept from a

---

1 Philip or George Wells, Winchester booksellers. The pamphlets referred to were those of the Society for Psychical Research disseminated by Russell's cousin.
2 The Oxford matriculation exam.

'priest' teaching they would reject from a layman. Still, I never really think the Church will be my destination.

Why do people want dogmas, and refuse to live without abstruse creeds? and why do they want to know everything, when they are quite as happy in reverent ignorance? I never felt the want of definite creeds, or of an anthropomorphic Saviour: I don't understand the need of them. If you want a powerful anti-clerical defence of the Godhead of Jesus, read Browning's 'Christmas Eve and Easter Day'; it is quite plain, and very powerfully put; the best thing about it being, that it leaves you to think what you like, without inflicting Church doctrine upon you; the poem comes in vol. 5 of his *Works*. I agree with you in thinking it improbable that Christ's teaching has been very materially perverted, it is generally easy to separate his own pure grain from the chaff his reporters mixed up with it. I cannot understand your view as to Paul being one of the initiated; to me, reading his Epistles and Myers' *St. Paul*,[1] it seems impossible to regard him otherwise than as an enthusiast for the divinity of Christ, with a metaphysical turn of mind. I won't show the book to anyone; I know of no one in College who would in the least appreciate it.[2] I must apologize for troubling you with so much illegibility. I have just come from Communion; I should not think much of a religion that had no such declaration of universal brotherhood. I will tell you my impressions of the book when I have got it.

---
1 F. W. H. Myers, *St Paul* (1863).
2 A. P. Sinnett, *Esoteric Buddhism* (1883).

Positivism I regard as the height of absurdity, infinitely worse in its bondage of dogma than the Catholic Church.

>I won't trouble you any further,
>Yrs affetly
>L. Johnson

P.S. As to exercise, I make no promise.

2

>College
>October 14, [1883]

Dear Russell,

I should have answered you before, but I have had too much to do. Doctor Ridding[1] told me yesterday I would become a proverb in the mouths of the printers' devils who had to read my MSS. I will now endeavour to remedy the defects in my last letter. Myer's [sic] *St. Paul* is a poem, analysing and stating Paul's views, in the shape of a soliloquy: it is well worth reading. Browning's poem I mentioned is called 'Christmas Eve and Easter Day'; to be found in volume five. I will attempt to solve the particular difficulty you mentioned, in Browning; Cantos V & VI, on page 171, briefly means this: the first opening study and reading of early Greek writings is simple enough, an 'outside frame' to the rest of Greek literature, as hazel

---

1 George Ridding (1828-1904), Headmaster of Winchester College, 1867-84. Known to Winchester boys as 'the Doctor'.

trees fringe a wood; but through Greek writings we see a wide passage opening out wider, till at last the study of Greek brings the reader to the thought and study of Italy and the Renaissance and the youth and new expansions of art and literature to be found there; and, although Italy is all the time a 'woman country', languid and effeminate in appearance, yet it has always had a strange attraction for men, e.g. Shelley, Byron; and so, Browning is willing to follow her leadership. You will find Browning's thought always simple; but the expression of the thought it somewhat hard; all the same, he is more worth mastering than any one else I know of. Mr Bradlaugh[1] is contemptibly vulgar; his logic, which is considerable, and his insensibility, which is incredible, have combined to produce clever but absolutely worthless books; he cannot have any real influence for good. I have none of his works; should burn them, if I had. To come to the real subject. I quite feel the sense of power and nobility in the Buddhist system: but it revolts me. I could not find any rest in a religion that required arithmetic and scientific knowledge. I have read carefully the first eight chapters; I have glanced at, but am about to read through, the rest. My position of mind with regard to them is this. I quite believe that the powers, &c, they assume, are real; that their lives are high in ideal; but that religion must be popular, not scientific. Were I alone in the world, such a life of abnegation and purity and absorption of self into deity, would be the ideal for me; but think of the people you meet

---

1 Charles Bradlaugh (1833-91), atheist and author of numerous works questioning religious doctrine.

every day, and then of that system! I am too essentially Western to appreciate Buddhism; it is true; but it is not, to speak technically, 'necessary for salvation';[1] i.e., a man may live the highest life, without it. I have an idea, that religion must vary under various circumstances; let the East keep its lofty ideal, and the West a simpler Christianity. I hate the very thought of degrees in religious questions; I hate the idea of any one patronising me, whether the head of the adepts, or an Evangelical parson. I have nothing to say against the religion of Buddha; it is an extremely noble one; but, as I said before, it repels me, chills me. I would rather be a Roman Catholic. Again, that this occult knowledge should have been in the world for ages, yet only intrusted to a few, is horrible; I can believe it all, but with the same kind of feelings with which I should regard a man who deliberately withheld an important discovery, because he thought the time had not come for revealing it. I hope I have not offended you with my comments on Buddhism; but it has not enough warmth and light and love, to satisfy me. The Dean preached a grand sermon today on the expansiveness and all embracingness of Christianity, which could shed its worn out dogmas as a snake does its skin. This all sounds rather Churchy, but I will not join the Church. I would rather not send you any of my productions; they are invisible to all but myself. Do read Browning; I feel much more cheerful about things in general when I have read him. Read, in the volume you are reading: 'Saul'; 'The Guardian Angel';

---

[1] Johnson is almost certainly quoting Russell back to himself, as he often did.

'Two in the Campagna'; 'Old Pictures in Florence'; and, above all, *'Evelyn Hope'*. You will understand them, with careful reading; and there is not one which will not inspire you with an ecstatic admiration and love of Browning, when you really see through it.

I apologize for this lengthy mass of illegibility.

Yrs affty

L. Johnson

3

College
October 16, [1883]

Dear Russell,

I have been hardly just towards Buddhism; the chapter on Nirvana is too transcendentally grand not to be a real, true ideal. But is it all practical? I mean, could the present world go on, if Buddhism and the struggles it entails were prevailing ideas? I admit that for those for whom it is possible, it is the supremist ideal; but is it not rather hard upon every day people, that they are placed, by no fault of their own, in situations in which this striving after the high state of spirituality would be impossible? Have you read Edwin Arnold's *Light of Asia*. I am reading it now, with inexpressible delight; but then, you see, it keeps the science in the background, and gives prominence to the spiritual side of the system. Who is Madam Blavatsky?[1] I keep hear-

---

1 Helena Petrovna Blavatsky (1831-91) co-founded the Theosophical Society with Henry Steel Olcott (1832-1907) and others in 1875.

ing allusions to her, and reading about her, as a mysterious personage, without the faintest idea as to who she is? Have you read *Mr. Isaacs*?[1] If so, what is meant by 'the groves of Simla, where Col: Olcott, Madam Blavatsky, and Mr. Sinnett perform their mysterious rites'?[2] The whole book is pervaded with allusions to the Adepts.[3] I read your book till about two o'clock last night, and then perambulated Chamber Court in the rain, to get my thoughts clear. I am entirely unable to get over my repugnance to the high tone of science and unspiritual knowledge that pervades the system; mathematics never yet were of any use for statesmen or religionists. But the idea of Nirvana (wh: I had grossly misunderstood before), is enough to convert the most determined Western sceptic. Do Buddhists practice celibacy? if so, it entails difficulties, and confirms what I said as to the impossibility of the religion of Buddha ever really spreading; it is true and good for those for whom it is possible; of whom I shall never be one, much though I should long to be. Excuse this disconnected discourse, but I wanted to apologize for any injustice my last letter might have done.

Yrs affly
L. Johnson.

---

1 F. Marion Crawford, *Mr. Isaacs: A Tale of Modern India* (1882).

2 By 1879, Simla (or Shimla), at the foothills of the Himalayas, was the home of A. P. Sinnett. He invited Madam Blavatsky there in 1880.

3 The term 'Adept' was widely used within Theosophy to describe those with a particularly high knowledge of Occultism; the highest being 'Master'.

Do read M. Arnold's *Literature and Dogma*; it throws a side light on Buddhism; a new edition is just out.

My clerical friend has just entreated me to 'consider whether I shld like to be in outer darkness with Buddha, or at the feet of Christ in perfect light.'!!

4

College
October 16, [1883]

Dear Russell,

I was glad and sorry to get your last letter; glad, because your partially recognizing my difficulties proves that they are not entirely the fault of my weak understanding; sorry, that I should have in any way disturbed your faith in Buddhism. A strange position, ours! two of young England's rising generation in search of a creed. I have come more or less to the conclusion that there is no absolute, universal Truth; that each of us has to struggle on, and make his Truth for himself. I can conceive of no religion which can equally satisfy me and a converted coal-heaver; again, abstract German metaphysics may and do attract and interest me, but I feel that they no more help me, than does Church of England orthodoxy. I quite know what you mean by an intense feeling of loathing and disgust and despair at things in general; once

I was late for names-calling,[1] because I had walked right away without knowing it to Bishopstoke.[2] But, whatever else may be doubtful, I feel certain that I am not in the world, with an individuality of my own, to be miserable; I am not responsible for my existence, and I have a right to be happy. Then, it follows that happiness is attainable, and, of course, of mind as well as, and more than, body. Then, I have a right to be happy; the means of happiness exists. I am unable to find it in established Churches, systems of thought &c; ergo, I must make it for myself. I have got as far as that, but, firstly, I do not know how to find my happiness; secondly, it seems selfish not to try and make other people's happiness as well; but I started by saying that my happiness depends upon (or, rather, my right to it depends upon), my own individuality; but I have no idea of other people's individualities; so that I am intrinsically selfish; ergo, miserable. So that I have been arguing in a circle, and wasting time. But it remains the fact, that I ought to be happy. Now that you have got six vols: of Browning, read 'Abt Vogler' in the fifth volume; it is, I think, intensely satisfying to people in our states of mind; in fact, Browning is my greatest consolation now. He studies and analyzes the soul, and drags it to light, and shows the good inherent in it and the nobility and comfort to be found even in trivial every day lives; in fact, 'the trivial round, the common task' &c.[3] But I think that the world itself, nature, will do for me to worship, if I

---

1 The Winchester equivalent of an attendance register.
2 A town seven miles south of Winchester.
3 John Kebel, 'Morning' in *The Christian Year* (1827).

can't find a God. I feel that I get more good by watching a peculiar sky, a colour in autumn trees, &c, than by hundreds of prayers. Of one thing I am certain; that I lived before I came into my present stage of existence, and that I shall live again; not, necessarily on this earth, or in the same personality, but again, somewhere, and somewhen. In the mean time, what Matthew Arnold calls 'morality' or 'conduct' will be a half guide. I would never willingly disturb another's faith, or try to pervert him to an absence of one. I can find spiritual food in nature as I said, in art, in poetry, in high ritual, in watching other people's characters; but these cannot make a Truth; my Christ is gone, and I cannot find another, or even the old one. I can't help writing to you; I must express what I think, it makes it all clearer to myself. But I will continue this tomorrow. My second letter may have explained my ideas more fully than the first, to which it was meant as a supplement.

October 18, 10.30.

Just got your letter; it seems partly to confirm what I have said as to the necessity of each one of us, according to our educated capacities, making his own happiness spiritually; but it does not solve the question of selfishness. A poor man of limited faculties often feels that the parson's orthodoxy and his grandmother's Christianity, do not meet his needs; he is unable to express his needs, but he feels them; then if you tell him that in 30 years he may attain to a high spiritual state, he would simply laugh at you. Buddhism may do for a few; but is it possible for people who, like myself, must work to get their living, in one way or another? I know that my unreasoning objections on the score of too much scientific technicality, to Buddhism, are not really of much weight; but if that was my only objection, I do not think it would influence me for a moment; but the impossibility of the religion's being carried out *in England by men who are of sufficient appreciation and culture to carry it out elsewhere*, appears to me an obstacle even to its limited diffusion. To come to earthly matters, I do take a great deal of exercise, for me; I am a member of the Shakespeare Society, and take leading female characters; I go out every day and declaim my part on Twyford Down. With repeated apologies for my persisting in writing.

Yrs afly
L. Johnson.

October 18, 7.30

Don't be alarmed; I shall finish this epistle some time or other. I begin to see; all this afternoon I walked round and round Hills,[1] reading the *Light of Asia*; the grandest poem I have read for years; it has made things clear: In its noble versified version of Buddha's first sermon, it distinctly states that ultimate perfection can be reached, even by those who cling to earthly ties, after a longer succession of trials and transmigrations; this is what I wanted. I think Christ must have meant this by his teaching, which is almost the same as Buddha's. The gospel of Buddha and Christ does

---

1 St Catherine's Hill, a mile south of Winchester College; a place where students took regular exercise.

teach a universal love, a tender sympathy for all men. You are unjust to Xtianity, when you say that it teaches that all the damned suffer equally; it is only rabid Protestants who do; the real, not unorthodox Xtianity, as the Broad Churchmen hold it, teaches that punishment is in limited degrees, and cannot be eternal. But, of course, none of this sort of thing is to be found in the New Testament. On maturer reflection, I do see that Buddhism is not more scientific than other systems. Art is intensely scientific; poetry has laws; Positivism is unbearably loaded with scientific dogma. Just as, in Xtianity, the life of Christ impels one to accept his teaching, so, to me, the life of Gautama[1] impels me to belief [in] him. Both men, or, perhaps, Gods are surrounded with a mass of legend; but the real personalities are gloriously distinct. I won't bore you any longer.

Yrs affly
L. Johnson.

P.S. I can't resist quoting a passage from my clerical friend; he says, 'Go into a dark room; light a candle; blow it out; feel the darkness round you; think of that as your heaven; for Nirvana is annihilation; whereas in Heaven, the vital spark of your soul will burn like an altar taper before the throne of God and all the blessed Saints.' I quote from memory; I have lost his letter; but I think that is correct.

---

1 Buddha.

5

College
October 21, [1883]

Dear Russell,

I have been formulating my yet remaining objections to Buddhism, and will briefly state them.

1. (This objection is only my old one stated in other words). Buddhism is, so to speak, too infinite; it compels you to throw your mind back and forward into boundless space and time, whilst the present insignificant world, or earth life, is full of untold misery; it was the sight, not of death only, but of mere human, bodily suffering, that induced Gautama Buddha to resign his station and love to win the Truth. I am certain that he, in his own mind and words, meant that the grand, spiritual Ideals and aims should be attainable by all, and the means of alleviating the mere temporary sufferings of this life. I know that you will not quite understand my insisting on this point; but when I spoke, before, of Happiness, I meant, of course, the happiness given even to human lives and comforts by a high spiritual life. I have a dim kind of answer to my own objections, but I will not state it.

2. The higher life of one who has entered on the path, forbids marriage; it is essential that a man should strive after the higher life; but, if he does, he dies, and the world is one man less, externally; then, why is man, as a corporeal animal, adapted for marriage, on the one hand, & for the higher life, on the other; you have no idea of what a frightful gulf of doubt this opens to me; I begin to doubt either the reality of the

grand series of world developments, or the justice of God, however you may define the word 'God'. Can it be, that this is so, that our faith and real aspiration may be tried, that the strength of our Karma may be realised? Even so, I think it is hard. You are wrong in supposing that I ever believed the old creeds; as a child, I never believed: my mind is essentially sceptical; so much so, that disbelief of anything other people tell me, or that I cannot see or prove, is sometimes a horrible mania. It is the sudden revelation of the possibilities of mankind in attaining to spiritual heights, even becoming Gods, that almost blinds me. I should like more intimate knowledge as to the state of mind and soul of the initiated; if they do really live in spirit. I have spent some time in carefully comparing the doctrines of Buddha, with the teaching of Christ; they almost coincide, allowing for local differences of time and occasion. As Buddha has been mistaken for God, in spite of his protests, so is Christ; both renounced their homes and quiet happiness to wander over their lands, to take away from death its sting, to teach us how to live; both have a gentleness and simplicity of character that draws all men unto them. I almost believe Christ was a re-incarnation of Buddha; at least, I see little reason against it. The successive incarnations we undergo, is perhaps meant to explain the apparent injustice I supposed, with regard to the entire purity enjoined on us. Those who cannot overcome the material tendencies of their natures in this life, will be strengthened in the next earth life. The fact is, that the whole system is so grand, that I cannot see it distinctly, if I come close to it, it is too colossal to be seen as a whole; if I look from a distance, its vast size makes it dim. I have no longer any real doubts as to its truth; my objections are merely defects of sight, which I shall overcome in time. Your cousin's letter is helpful;[1] I do not feel, as I thought I should, that the idea of immutable Law is chilling; I see that mutable Law would be miserable and unsatisfactory; whilst salvation goes on always, and God is everywhere. The doctrine cannot, of course, be the same to all; but it presents all with that particular aspect wh: suits him best. And the especial nobility lies in its sublime disregard of those who do not openly profess to believe it, or who have never heard of it; it has the stamp of natural greatness on it. I will read the book through again, more carefully, and state what further objections to it I can find. With regard to 'Abt Vogler', ix, x, xi, are the stanzas that contain the meaning: simple enough, as all his important parts always are. I like the Parody; it is forcible. I knew Maclagan[2] had the *Light of Asia*; he has not read it. Was at Lady Laura's for lunch;[3] Salvation Army chief topic of conversation; the Doctor enthusiastic for it.

Yrs affly,
L. Johnson.

---

1 St George Lane Fox-Pitt (1856-1932), who had introduced Russell to Buddhism.
2 Edward Douglas Maclagan (1864-1952), future Indian civil servant and historian.
3 Lady Laura Ridding (1849-1939), the Headmaster's wife.

6

College
October 22, [1883]

Dear Russell,

I have at last satisfactorily solved for myself the marriage difficulty. In my view of the question, the justice of God, unwilling to limit the number of those who might ultimately attain to Nirvana, has permitted and enjoined marriage, as a means of increasing the number of the 'saved'; since the married in one earth-life, need not be married in the next; and, of course, marriage is not sin in itself. I am now quite reconciled to Buddhism, so far as I understand it. Its special nobility seems to me to be this; that, whereas orthodox Christians can go on in a slip-shod way, trusting to death-bed repentance and priestly absolution, in Buddhism, as your cousin says, every act is a cause; every step in life, every word and thought and deed is of the utmost importance. This strikes me as the supreme height of moral grandeur. I know Mill's book on Comte, well;[1] very clever, but hardly fair: Myers' *Essays* are delightful;[2] everything is, that he writes. Do you attempt at all to propagate the gospel of Gautama? Most men at Oxford are like St. Paul's Athenians; ready for some new thing; but ridiculing anything that contradicts their shallow philosophies.

Waterfield is fairly well, but has been continent;[3] I

---

1 John Stuart Mill, *Auguste Comte and Positivism* (1865).
2 F. W. H. Myers, *Essays Classical* and *Essays Modern* (1883).
3 Reginald Waterfield (1867-1967), future Principal of Cheltenham College and Dean of Hereford. To be or go 'continent' meant to be confined to the sick-house.

have told him to write. I think that Buddhism should be preached openly, with care; the idea of secrecy and initiation are alien to English minds. I wish I knew more about the Elementals; it is one of Cardinal Newman's ideas that the operations of nature are carried on by invisible yet real agencies. I am carefully reading and digesting the doctrine of *Esoteric Buddhism*; it is very noble.

Yrs affly,
L. Johnson

Excuse my execrable scrawl; am in hurry.

7

College
November 2, [1883]

Dear Russell,

I shall be delighted to exert myself to an unwonted extent next Tuesday afternoon with you. I am absolutely confirmed in my Buddhism by reading Plato, whom study in Jowett's version;[1] Plato distinctly describes the system of 'world chains and planetary evolutions', in his own limited phraseology; and he gives an entirely accurate description of the state of Devachan and the conditions there of souls with vary-

---

1 Benjamin Jowett, *The Dialogues of Plato in five volumes* (1871). At the time of these letters Jowett (1817-93) was Master of Balliol College and Vice-Chancellor of the University of Oxford.

ing degrees of Karma;[1] he describes exactly the upward spiral process of the worlds; and when he is about to speak of these things, he invariably introduces them with the words, 'these things I learnt from a certain man'; once, 'this I was told by Er the Armenian, who was enabled to return to earth from death.' He speaks of Socrates as having a personal 'Δαίμων'[2] at his ear, who told him what to teach. Plato is quite convincing. Acting up to the creed is, of course, immensely difficult; but time works wonders. I have no more time just now, so, till Tuesday, vale![3]

Yrs affly,
L. Johnson

Yesterday, in an essay for the Doctor on Religious Persecution, I dragged in a tolerably clear statement of Buddhism, expressing my personal views on the subject; I expect to be sat upon accordingly.

8

College
November 11, [1883]

Dear Russell,

Just returned from Cathedral, where heard excel-

---

[1] In *Esoteric Buddhism*, Sinnett describes Devachan as a state, rather than locality, where a soul waits to be reborn; a state of introspection varying for each individual, befitting his spiritual development to ready him for his next human existence.
[2] Daimōn or daemon.
[3] Farewell.

lent sermon from Judge's Chaplain.[1] I tried to get hold of the Daker yesterday;[2] he was watching our victory over Houses;[3] but he disappeared; but I am thinking of going to St. John's tonight, in which case I will ask him about the cat.[4] I have had no further communications from the Doctor on the subject of Buddhism. I should like to see his paper on Purity very much:[5] the newspapers give it an unintelligible form: the other address you mention sounds disagreeable, but I should like to see it, if it is not too much trouble to you. Mrs. J.[6] has been gushing to me about you, but I did not give her your address; said I was not quite sure of it; but she did want to have it. My clerical friend has, since his last epistle, prepared an elaborate essay on the 'Essential Genius of Protestant Christianity, as Contrasted with the False Doctrines of Oriental Superstition'. Having digested this Leviathan of a title, I read the MS: and returned it with thanks. It was the most foul-mouthed slander I ever read: it was abominable in its superficial assumption of su-

---

1 The assize sermon that morning was preached by the High Sheriff of the County's chaplain, Revd William Norman.
2 'Daker' was the nickname of Revd Henry Compton Dickins (1838-1920), former tutor at the school and by then vicar at St. John's, Winchester.
3 The annual fifteen-a-side football tournament (known as 'Fifteens') played by different parts of the school. The College team played Houses on 10 November 1883, winning 5-2.
4 When Russell visited Winchester on 6 November he rescued a half-drowned cat and took it to the Daker to nurse.
5 George Ridding, *Purity, a paper*, delivered to the 23rd Church Congress, Reading, Berkshire, 3 Oct 1883.
6 Most probably 'Mrs Jahra', the nickname for Lady Laura, Dr Ridding's wife.

periority. I quote one sentence: 'If absolute annihilation is the end of existence, why not at once commit suicide?' He also said, when I advised him to read *Esoteric Buddhism*, that he was afraid of 'touching the unclean thing'. I don't believe in Morris as a practical politician; he is the moving spirit of the Democratic Federation, which stamps him as Utopian; but he is an intense enthusiast, and worth listening to.[1] I shall certainly think again about trying for Balliol; but I am not a scholar, only an individual of literary tastes.

Yrs affly,
L. Johnson.

I am quite aware that I have told you nothing worth telling; but I like inflicting my epistles on people.

9

College
November 13, [1883]

Dear Russell,

Much obliged for the pamphlets; have seen *Outcast London* before, but glad to read it again.[2] The Doctor is very good; so exceedingly refined, and, at the same time outspoken. I think you had better take the other

---

1 William Morris delivered a controversial speech at the Russell Club, Oxford on 14 Nov 1883 which Russell attended. See letter 10.
2 London Congregational Union, *The Bitter Cry of Outcast London: an enquiry into the condition of the abject poor* (1883).

paper to heart, if you intend to make a habit of tea drinking at 2.30 a.m. Mrs Dick[1] has been pouring out her motherly fears for you to me; she wanted to know why you had changed so, and were so remarkably melancholy; I felt obliged to enlighten her, a little, on the subject of Buddhism, speaking of it lightly as your latest fancy; she entreats me to discourage you; I said I would do my best; I hope my slight unveracities won't be visited upon me! The Daker preached a glorious sermon at St. John's last Sunday evening; he demolished St. Augustine, Socinus, Luther, Alford, and the Bishop of Bedford, declaring that the words 'Be ye perfect, as your Father is perfect' meant what they said, i.e., that man is a potential God; in fact, he unconsciously preached pure Buddhism. There are a swarm of old Wykehamists down here, who beat us this morning: no one, except Vidal,[2] whom I care for at all. Thanks for what you told me of Jowett's sermon: it must have been beautiful; but, to my irreverent mind, there is something ludicrous in the idea of Jowett meeting Pusey in Heaven. We have just finished the *Phaedo* with the Dr: it is almost too pathetic to keep from tears. Compare the death of Socrates with that of Jesus; both are equally sublime. I speak tonight on Capital Punishment; good subject, but rather worn out. We had an excellent sermon

---

[1] Sarah Richardson (1842-1909), wife of Second Master Revd George Richardson (1839-1904), affectionately known to the boys as 'Dick'.
[2] George Studley Sealy Vidal (1862-1928), then at New College and afterwards tutor at St Mary's Hall.

from Randell,[1] a man who examines, in Chapel last Sunday; I like his last words: 'It is very hard to live by faith in the unseen; I only know one thing harder—to live without it.' Maclagan told me your speech at the Union was a distinct success;[2] but he at once asked me if I knew anything about your new religion, rather to my surprise: I suppose you have been propounding it to him. I am writing now, because I want to waste time, to give a polite reason. Have you seen Arthur Lillie's book, *Popular Life of Buddha*, with an answer to Rhys David's Hibbert Lectures on Buddhism?[3] it is a good book, but written in superlatives and italics. I have shirked Chapel for two days running, now, a flagrant enormity in my eyes, but not in Ridding's; he asked me, sarcastically, this morning, if I thought Nirvana was the same as lying in bed; I told him it was very like it, only more so; he remarked, that my definition of Nirvana was as lucid as most people's, but that that was not saying much.

Yrs affl,
L. Johnson.

---

1 This name was difficult to decipher, but possibly Johnson refers to Thomas Randell (1849-1915), Anglican cleric, then studying theology at St John's, Oxford; a licensed preacher in the Oxford diocese who shortly afterwards became an examiner in theology at Bede College, Durham, a training college for masters.
2 Russell spoke at the Oxford Union against field sports on 1 Nov 1883.
3 Arthur Lillie, *The Popular Life of Buddha containing an answer to the 'Hibbert Lectures' of 1881* (1883).

10

College
November 17, [1883]

Dear Russell,

I hasten to dispel any illusion on your part as to my opinion on the subject of your melancholy, as distinct from Mrs. R's.[1] I don't consider you so, because I understand more of your internal state; but people who know nothing of any mental or spiritual process of change in you, may very naturally take its external manifestations to be a kind of melancholy gloom. William Morris's lecture, as reported by the papers, struck me as very good; but neither he nor Ruskin, though I almost worship them both, seem to me practical in any sense. I harangued Debating Society on the subject of Capital Punishment last Tuesday; all my eloquence only obtained four votes as against fifteen; but several Dons expressed to me their regret at not having votes, as they would have given them for me. Next Thursday I defend belief in disembodied spirits; I really must enlighten the House a little on the subject. I am writing this from Sick House, where I am nourishing a youth sublime,[2] i.e., a sore throat, with a view to being able to read at the Shakespeare Reading tonight. Have you seen the last *Trusty Servant*?[3] the criticisms on the Society have

1 Mrs Richardson, i.e. Mrs Dick.
2 Alfred, Lord Tennyson, 'Locksley Hall' (1842), 'Here about the beach I wander'd, nourishing a youth sublime'.
3 *The Trusty Servant* was a short-lived magazine (April 1883—July 1884), established by a group of boys to rival the long-standing school magazine, *The Wykehamist*.

driven Mr Hawkins frantic; he harangued the Society last night for half an hour, went to the Dr: to get it sconced officially, sympathised with me over 'that disgustingly unjust piece of impertinent criticism' which concerned me—in short, he is out of his senses on the subject.[1] Do you know Lewis Morris at all? if not, do read his new book, *Songs Unsung*, and peruse a poem called the 'New Creed'. Did I ever tell you a strange kind of dream I had a few months ago? I was sleeping quietly, when I felt a shock go right through me, and I seemed to have left my body behind, and gone off to the stars; I saw myriads of lights streaming over and on a vast white lake; I was in a state of perfect ecstasy, when I felt myself whirled back to my body, and woke up with a violent sense of splitting headache; I at once got up, while the impression was fresh and vivid, and wrote down an exact record of my impressions in a poem; it is now somewhat unintelligible, but absolutely accurate as a faithful record of immense sensations and influences. I never experienced any thing like it before or since. I have no time to copy it out legibly, but send it you as it was written. The other poems are not to the point.

Yrs affly
L. Johnson.

A DREAM

One night far up amongst the white stars dreaming
I knew my soul wafted away from me,

---

1 Charles Halford Hawkins (1838-1900), Mathematical Master at Winchester and co-founder of the Shakespeare Society. 'Sconce' means to hinder or obstruct.

To where a clear coruscant light was gleaming
And shot forth rays across a stilly sea.

The air was laden with a chilly numbness
And then my soul felt sudden iron hands
Strike through her utterance a thrill of dumbness
And gird her round with thwarting steely bands.

She moved not, neither knew the fateful region
Only the glare of white eye-dazzling rays,
Only the blue, dark sea, and many a legion
Of fluttering stars and spirits of unknown days.

These only marked she and with timid wonder
Gazed upon hosts of alternating light;
And ever and anon the scene asunder
Was cleft by radiance of higher might.

Faint with much straining of her eyes, she inward
Turned them, and in her secret self she mused,
Whether she now were feebly staring sinward
And her true seeing ruthlessly abused.

Or if to glories of the highest heaven
These fitful blinding darts guided the way;
And iron bands for strengthening staves were given
And she were gazing in the sunward day.

While thus she mused, she felt a stirring motion
Of tossing surges, and of restless seas;
And turning toward the sound, the purple ocean
She saw besprinkled with pale phantasies.

And to her eyes their form was as of strangers
That know not where to turn nor how to rest,
And hover listlessly o'er quaking dangers
And fain would sleep upon a serpent's breast.

Then as she downward gazed upon them lying,
Around her flowed a sea of shimmering light
And countless images she saw, all flying
Down to the waves with headlong wings of flight.

And as they touched the waters, straight a terror
Of frantic billows, and clashing tides,
And currents seized in multitudinous error,
And all was noise, where nought of rest abides.

No more she knew, but when her aching senses
Once more were quickened then in wondering wise
She felt herself a part of piercing lenses
Through which all things were seen by fearful eyes.

A weird expansion felt she of her nature,
Whereby she shared in all the world around
And she became a part of every creature
And was transfused in every sight and sound.

Yet still she hung aloft in starry places
And felt the floods of light upon her life;
But of the sea were gone all heaving traces,
And only light clove light in dazzling strife.

White stars marched on and on in high procession,
And æons came with steps of stately feet;
And in the heavenly arc was no transgression,
And moons still rose and sank, still silver sweet.

Only a quickening current stirred the spirit
Of life, and self died from the range of things,
A brother's love was each man's to inherit,
And soul met soul with other seeking wings.

The vision fled before my eyelids waking
And to the glare succeeded blinding night
As back to earth her way my soul was taking
And the sun rose upon the face of night.

I care not greatly for the stress of anguish
But ah! that I might pierce the veil that shrouds
The unseen world, that I no more might languish
With eyes that ache to cleave the heavy clouds.

Thus once I cried but now I cry no longer,
To send my soul to realms of eterne light,
Heaven's rays than my poor soul are ever stronger,
And heavenly stars too strong for my poor sight.

July 1883

11

College
November 20, [1883]

Dear Russell,

I must apologise for having detained your pamphlets so long, but I had forgotten their existence; I will send them off today. The articles in the *Wykehamist* are the productions of Lumby and Fort;[1] the criticism on the debate, as well as that in the *Trusty* are the work of Talbot,[2] who simply loathes me; I return the compliment. I wrote that somewhat illucid poem just when I was under the spell of having discovered in *St. Paul* a new metre; I have used it largely since then, but it is rather artificial. I have performed a heroic act; I yesterday spent an hour in arranging my papers; and I burned my earliest extant productions; they were twenty sonnets written in October last year; so that my present MSS are the poetical fruits of this year only; they amount to about a hundred close written sheets of long paper: I wrote a beautiful sonnet descriptive of my emotions on seeing my offspring burning, which consoles me for their loss; they were certainly too immature to deserve life. Mrs. Dick's report ought to be interesting; I almost ridiculed Buddhism to her. By the way, I must renounce all claim to many of the absurd statements on Capital Punishment attributed to me; they are purely Talbot's invention. Talbot is the kind of clever man I hate; very clever and even

---

[1] John Rawson Lumby (1865-1941), later a journalist; James Alfred Fort (1859-1934), master at Winchester and president of the Debating Society.
[2] Bertram Chetwynd Talbot (1865-1936).

brilliant, but incredibly superficial and showy; he will make a shrewd party politician or magazine writer.[1] I rather disagree with you as to St. Paul's character; I take him to be an intensely mystical enthusiast; a kind of early Ignatius Loyola or General Booth; very practical and hard working, but still passionately mystic and introspective, with a taste for dogmatic theology: I don't see that Myers really presents him as contemplative. I know the essay on Renan well; it was Benson's favourite in the series.[2] I have lately been writing sonnets on Buddha; not of any value, except as real expressions of personal feeling. I spoke to the Daker yesterday on the subject of our cat, but he professed entire ignorance of the incident, but promised to make inquiries. Gladstone was very good in a simple way down here; spoke a few kind words very earnestly; it does one good to hear the man speak; he impresses me with such a sense of reverence.[3] I am writing in a hurry, and under the unpleasant feeling of having to answer questions for the Doctor on Roman literature of the silver age, which I have absolutely not got up at all. Are you coming down for Sixes?[4]

Yrs affetly
L. Johnson

I had heard of Jowett's calligraphy; it looks characteristic of the man.

---

1 Talbot became neither, but was a clerk in the House of Commons from 1888-1903.
2 Godfrey Rathbone Benson (1864-1945), later author, liberal politician and philanthropist, was then at Balliol with Russell.
3 Prime Minister William Ewart Gladstone (1809-98) visited Winchester College on 19 Nov 1883.
4 The annual six-a-side football contest.

12

College
November 25, [1883]

Dear Russell,

I hope your pamphlets have arrived by this time: I certainly gave them to porter some days ago, to post; I will inquire as to their fate. I cannot say how thankful I am for the last pamphlet; it does entirely dispose of many little burning doubts I could not entirely get rid of; though, as you say, I hardly need conversion so much as further instruction. How can I live at all conformably here, even in externals? I can't possibly practice vegetarianism, and I feel that I am wasting time. I have not destroyed all my MSS; only my early sonnets, about twenty; I have still a formidable quantity of lyrics and sonnets, with longer poems. I succeeded in mystifying the House completely on the subject of Spirits; I am rather looking forward to the report of what I did not say in the *Wykehamist*; all the same, ghosts do exist by 18 to 5! rather a practical triumph for them. I hardly know why, but I do feel lazy; however, the Dr: complemented me effusively on my remarks on Roman Lit: which speaks greatly for my imaginative powers. I don't envy you your exams: scholarship is a delusion; 'culture' is the real thing. I have just inquired of porter as to the pamphlets; he remarked that he has seen 'quite haccidental, Sir', Dr. Ridding's paper: and he felt bound to read it; he hoped no offence, and sent them off again last night:

pretty cool of him. At one period of my life I called myself a Swedenborgian: very few people know how wonderfully great a man he was. Is there any truth in the statement as to Alexandria and the sacred books? if so, why could not the Buddhists have altogether exerted their powers over the fire? Perhaps the reason was political. Who is the author of the pamphlet, or rather the answer to the Swedenborgian? he is severe upon poor Olcott for his Americanisms. I wish you joy of your interview with a real live Buddhist.[1]

Yrs affly
L. Johnson

13

College
[November 30, 1883]

Dear Russell,

Your letter reads, to me, just like an extract from my own remarks on ghosts; I mean, as to belief being not capable of intellectual demonstration to unbelievers, being in itself an intuition. I certainly hold that many people are unconscious Bhuddists,[2] who would reject with laughter the definite dogmas of *Esoteric Bhuddism*; so that it is very necessary not to bring forward too prominently the externals of the Esoteric doctrine; i.e., not to lay much stress on the Brotherhood, on so-called supernatural powers, but

---

1 The unidentified Buddhist was expected to join Russell for tea that day, but never came.
2 It is unclear why Johnson chooses this spelling occasionally.

rather on the inner personal morality of the doctrine; at least, so I have found down here, when trying to explain things to a few people who have accidentally seen any of your pamphlets. I have sent on your *Hints* to Miss Stanley:[1] many thanks for them. I have been thinking a good deal lately about a systematic study of Oriental languages; but I have no natural gift for languages, and am rather despairing. I find a good many Dons know all about it: Hardy[2] was talking in the most painfully unappreciative way the other day about Madam Blavatsky's book.[3] I have lately taken to reading the Bible as pure literature; Isaiah is very like Aeschylus. I am now in the agony of exam, or rather of preparation for it, so have little time to spare: I congratulate you on your success.[4] Did you read in the papers the account of these Siamese proceedings and ceremonies? it struck me as significant that the King of Siam's envoy, his brother, and the minister, in addressing Siamese students over here, said that their only hope of succeeding was in keeping the Bhuddist religion pure?[5] it sounded encouraging to me, coming from highly civilized Orientals. I wish I had more time here at my own disposal; at present I find classical drudgery very exacting, when I want to think quietly. We have a Confirmation tomorrow; significant insti-

---

1 Maude Alethea Stanley (1833-1915), Russell's maternal aunt.
2 Henry John Hardy (1860-1939), later a master at Winchester.
3 *Isis Unveiled* (1877).
4 Russell sat scholarship exams between 24 and 28 November 1883 but was unsuccessful.
5 Prince Prisdang, envoy of the King of Siam, held a dinner in London for dignitaries and Siamese students on 27 November 1883.

tution, utterly perverted. Read St. John's Gospel carefully; it is very beautiful and instructive, and comes from an intensely spiritualized man. Swedenborg is a simply mesmeric force to some people: he exercises a most wonderful fascination: I know two ladies who worship him, literally, thinking him an incarnation of Deity: an unorthodox doctrine for Swedenborgians. Max Müller[1] never seems to be an attractive man from his books; he will make out everything to be a solar myth, and destroys all the poetry of classical and Scandinavian tradition. I am glad that you have come round to reasonable views on Vivisection: but Gautama gives a higher ground than yours:

> 'Kill not—for Pity's sake; and lest ye slay
> The meanest thing upon its upward way.'[2]

Pity, you see, comes first; and remember, too, his words about sacrifices and animal slaughter generally. I wish Burdon Sanderson was at the bottom of the sea—anywhere rather than in Oxford.[3] Fisher, of Du Boulay's house, gave us a most excellent speech on ghosts; but he is an exclusively intellectual man, too proud of his intellect to keep it in the background at all.[4] I do think that great things might be done at

---

1 [Friedrich] Max Müller (1823-1900), philologist, Sanskritist and curator of the Bodleian Library, 1856-63 and 1881-94. Russell was his frequent guest in 1883-4.
2 Edwin Arnold, *The Light of Asia* (1879).
3 John Burdon-Sanderson (1828-1905), Doctor of Medicine and physiologist, was appointed Waynflete Professor of Physiology in 1883. His inaugural speech on the Study of Physiology on 22 October 1883 contained strong pro-vivisection views.
4 Herbert Albert Laurens Fisher (1865-1940), later a historian,

Oxford, with patience; if an exposition of the pure ethics of the system fails, then, let men believe 'for the very works' sake';[1] but to get any belief at all implies a gradual ascent in belief, irresistibly. Could not a Society of some kind be formed there under the superintendence of the Theosophical Society? it would not bring forward sacred things, of course, prominently, but simply offer any one a chance of examining the truth of Bhuddism, if only from the intellectual point of view; even that does some good, by exposing the weakness of intellect. But perhaps individual work is more effective, for the present; and even common place undergrads have more earth-lives than Xtianity offers them.

Yrs afftly
L. Johnson

Excuse writing; am in middle of Chorus of *Agamemnon*; the third chorus is Hellenically presented Bhuddism. Aeschylus was inspired.

14

King's Mead, Windsor Forest[2]
[December 20, 1883]

Dear Russell,
Your letter is a very natural one in many ways;[3]

---

was a commoner in 'C' House. The Master of his house was Revd J. T. H Du Boulay (1832-1915).
1 John 14:11, 'or else believe me for the very works' sake'.
2 The Johnsons' family home.
3 Johnson responds to Russell's appeal for 'comfort and

I know so well by personal experience, though you might not think it, how hard the struggle after spirituality is. I often, even now, feel that my aspirations are not enough of a reality to have a permanent influence; I know their truth and grandeur, in the abstract, and all the while find myself drifting along at pleasure, almost content to have it so. No, I don't think that either you or I deliberately live the lower life; I think that this anguish of remorse, which I feel, as well as you, for you have not known me long, is only the result of true attempts to live the higher; if you were really living entirely basely, you would soon renounce the ideal. As soon as we attain and realize our ideals, and we think we are successful, then, Browning teaches, we have really failed, because the essence of an Ideal is that it should not be a thing capable of being realized to the full, but only an aim placed above our reach, only to be *won* by *endless* striving. Every sin, every unspiritual thought, is an awful cause of consequences; but the feeling of remorse is the beginning of higher things.—I could go on for ever in this way, but I have said enough. My personal feelings are to some extent those of anger with myself for my blindness; I have always been trying to find a philosophy of soul and sense which should unite the two; the result always being, the subjection of the former; now, of course I see how utterly mistaken I was, and how infinitely harder I have made it, to break the ties of the latter and free my spirit altogether. I

---

encouragement' following his 'jaw' from George Richardson and chastisement by his grandmother for 'proselytizing' Johnson, as described in the Introduction.

don't think we are conceited: people often say I am; I always analyze my feelings, and I have resolved the conceit, not, I hope, conceitedly, into self-consciousness and impatience, trying to hide themselves. And, if I appear conceited to others, God knows I know my own littleness, too well. To come, for a short time, to other affairs. Joseph and I are bracketed for the Moore Stevens Divinity Prize; that was the meaning of my St. John paper; I believe there is an idea of putting it off till the summer, on the understanding that we are to be given it, then.[1] Also, I was fourth in New Exam, and been loaded with Spooner's congratulations.[2] So that, in worldly matters, I am successful enough; my Plato paper, full of Buddhism, got highest marks. I feel rather ill, just now; I walked ten miles last night in the Forest at midnight to clear my brain, and am very tired. I don't think I shall be in town for any time just now. I think, if it is not in yr way, I shd prefer your keeping Mallock till I go back to Winchester.[3] Luke = Matthew Arnold, a perfect portrait in every way. You must have heard of Professor Clifford,[4] an intensely

---

1 Johnson did not win the prize: it went to Horace William Brindley Joseph (1867-1943) later a Philosopher, Tutor, and Senior Proctor at New College, Oxford.
2 New College, Oxford, began as the senior foundation to Winchester College. Five scholarships and two exhibitions were awarded each year as a result of the New Exam. William Archibald Spooner (1844-1930) was the New College don whose absentmindedness and supposed muddling of syllables in spoken phrases gave rise to the term *spoonerisms*.
3 Identified from Russell's journal as W. H. Mallock, *The New Republic* (1877).
4 William Kingdon Clifford (1845-79), mathematician and philosopher.

brilliant young mathematician at Oxford, who used to write whole libraries in a superior Bradlaughlite style; he was a friend of your father, I know, and wonderfully fascinating and enthusiastic; his early death was a frightful loss to literature and philosophy: he was the very antithesis to our beliefs, and worshipped intellect and reason. I think I shall be able to go to Balliol at Easter; I should be delighted, and my people will do anything for me, if I put it persuasively enough. I got here yesterday to find them all at Mass, and they are all at Church now. It is so strange to live in a world of intense faith! there is some thing so grand in the idea of limitless faith in the unseen, and distrust in the seen and the reasoned. I have great fears for our religion, all the same; did you see an article in that abominable paper *Truth*, on 'Buddhism, the fashionable craze', as the latest fashion, just like sham aestheticism? The number of people who profess Buddhism astonishes me, when I consider that so few try and live up to their professions. But, still, truth must prevail in the end. I think that the frame of mind in which people commit suicide is one which is to be cultivated; I mean, that longing to have done with the things of world and precipitate oneself into the illimitable vacancy of death: for then we can really rise above the desire for death, by dying, as Paul says, daily in the flesh. Of course, the flesh resists, is meant to resist, by its nature; of course, we must sometimes fall, and keep the memory of the fall; but yet, as I have said, the state of remorse is a higher state. And it is possible to over estimate the extent of the past fall and disgrace; it [is] often wise to leave the past, to itself, and yearn forwards into the future. For every act of unspirituality—the best word, being negative, as all sin is—let an act of spiritual intention, if not attainment, be set as an atonement. The light is not given to throw its rays into the past night; it brightens the dawn, and continues to rise until it reach the zenith; it sinks, in nature, but not in the supernatural. So we need not really despair, because of accusing memories; rather, let us leave them alone, and create fresh ones. I can't write any more just at present

Yrs affectionately
L. Johnson

Excuse writing.

15

King's Mead, Windsor Forest
[December 30, 1883]

Dear Russell,

Excuse my long silence, especially as it is only broken now by a preface to a longer. My father, acting on letters from the Doctor and Second Master,[1] has forbidden me to correspond with you, and requests you to abstain from writing to me. The people at Winchester have no real knowledge of our thoughts, and insist upon the 'unhealthiness' of such religious discussion. Well, of course at home I can't thoroughly

---

1 The Second Master (George Richardson) acted as housemaster to the section of the school known as 'College', to which Johnson belonged.

explain myself, and so I can only submit in silence. Don't suppose that our friendship is in any way broken, though it is thwarted by others with good intentions. You see, my father simply talks of Theosophists as 'a pack of idiotic fools', and thinks our having views of our own sheer nonsense, so he views you as a clever individual, whose brain is full of cobwebs, whose friendship is pernicious to me, as a Christian. I do not attempt to argue the point, and merely gave my word to abstain from correspondence. It will not really hurt us, perhaps only strengthen us. The Winchester people both pointed at my influence being pernicious, from a religious point of view, to the school, and suggested that if I did not get clear of these ideas and habits of solitude, I should have to leave; well, it may come to that, but I can't say. I think I shall really care for the things of the body more, as you advise, and make up for want of religious sympathy by practical wisdom in the way of exercise. My people are very much in earnest in what they say, and really regard you as a most deadly influence. Your people are more liberal, but even they do not sympathize. 'Excuse these wild and wandering thoughts',[1] but I am in a hurry, and rather ill. My faith will perhaps be soon tested; the Second Master says, practically, 'Either leave the school, or be in harmony with it'; the Dr. says, 'I think there is something in you, and that something may come of all your mental anxieties, but it is not an edifying

---

1 From the prelude to Tennyson's *In Memoriam* (1850) quoted from memory: 'Forgive these wild and wandering cries, / Confusions of a wasted youth; / Forgive them where they fail in truth, / And in thy wisdom make me wise'.

sight for the school, so be quick about it.' That is the state of the case, so farewell till—Nirvana, as far as I can see!

Ever yrs,
L. Johnson.

16

College
February 8, [1884]

Dear Sayle,[1]

Thank you: that is the most expressive phrase that my mind in its present state of bewilderment can suggest. I think that this state of separation and isolation which is forced upon me makes me very egotistical; I feel as if I could only write or think of my own wretched self, whereas the less I think at all the better it will be eventually. I am not coherent, but it is inevitable. You are no stranger to me, if anything of similarity of thought can, as it must, do away with the want of conventional acquaintance.

Again I thank you: it is indeed cheering to feel that the world is very large and any given society in it very minute: I find it a comfort in a kind of vague recognition of the numberless dead and the many living who are our spiritual brothers. I don't think that I am violating any promise or understanding between

---

1 Charles Edward (Charlie) Sayle (1864-1924) at New College, Oxford. Russell wrote of Sayle in his diary of 4 February 1884: 'it is marvellous how that man spreads the milk of human kindness'. This letter suggests he extended that goodwill to Johnson following the ban on correspondence with Russell.

myself and my immediate superiors in writing to you; thought and intuition are unfettered except by our selves, and I am but thinking and pondering to others instead of to myself. Give Russell my love; I know what he must feel about our state, and how real a test of sincerity it is. Tell him to read Browning's *Paracelsus*; I have just now bathed myself in its living waters, and feel that the truth is very true, and that many failures only mean that it is worth the struggle. But I will not even in word seem to break my promise; I will only think to myself of him, and wait. Strange, the link that sympathy is to what the world calls 'strangers'! I know very little of you, as you of me; but I have no hesitation in feeling that we are not strangers. Yes, I think I can claim pity; but then, these things are but 'mortalia', and the light of truth is deathless, even to the wiping away of kindly tears. I find, now, most pleasure of spirit in mere daily life, the 'common round' which Christianity fails so piteously to imbue with the spirit of Christ; in poor efforts at higher life of action, a change from passive unrest of thought to truer activity of life prompted by thought. Ah, the treasures of nature, the untold richness of literature, which I discover *now*, in before unguessed profusion! perhaps it is in this expansion of the intellectual enjoyment together with absolute suppression of intellectual pride, that the Truth has its chiefest glory. Pardon me these mere effusions of egotism; you can not conceive the happiness of expressing the heart's real thought, of getting it away, so to speak, of really feeling the ecstasy of truth. Tell Russell, if you will, that I am never forgetful of his having been the chosen minister to me of the truth, that I am really with him in spirit. Again I thank you for your kindness, and will ever be

Yrs affecly
L. Johnson

17

College
February 11, [1884]

Dear Sayle,

I have received, read, and appreciated the *Leaflet*.[1] I would rather not appear insincere by criticizing your share in it, so will only ask you who wrote a little poem you do not claim; but which has wonderfully impressed me,—though more by what it suggests than expresses—I mean the song with the burden, 'Ah, me! the journey is long'?[2] I think the paper a decided step in the right direction, though a little discursive in scope. But I proceed to your letter. I knew you would quarrel with me for placing sympathy amongst the things that perish; perhaps my point of view is too exclusively individual for others to recognize; I have always thought that personal affection and mere affinity of taste are too much, if I may talk Browning, of successes not to be failures and evidences of short coming: I have always yearned to be able to greet all

---

[1] The literary paper started by Sayle, John Badley and others at Rugby School ran from May 1883-April 1887.
[2] The poem entitled 'We Cannot Know' was in fact written by Sayle and appeared in December 1883.

men as my brothers instinctively, not by accident of 'juxtaposition'. But, none the less, I do see in love of such a limited kind enough evidence of dissatisfaction with itself, to warrant my regarding it as a reaching upwards, an attempt at supplying the frame with a picture, completing the incompleteness of things.

I am not altogether sorry at being unable to read Bhuddist literature: I feel a kind of repulsion towards the mere knowledge of which they seem so proud, not because it is a help towards revealing spiritual truth, but simply as elevating them above 'Western Scientists'. Surely, truth is not absolute in form as well as in essence? surely Swedenborg and the medieval German mystics are as really in possession of spiritual truth adapted to their needs, as are the Oriental adepts of the truth in its more impressive, because less questioned hitherto, form? All men do reach the absolute truth some time: all men are 'saved' or 'lost', though aeons hence: that, at least, we owe as a fact capable of demonstration to the East; so that if I, as a Western, living amongst Western people, subject to local limitations of custom and possibility, do none the less dimly apprehend and earnestly strive after the light which lighteth every man, coming into the world:—then, I claim to be living the highest life possible for me and such as I, though, God knows, painfully falling short of the highest ideal.

Oh, that I knew what my lot in life is to be! if only I might ever guess at myself, as I shall go into the grave! I am very much in need of counsel, through unfortunate misconceptions of my real feelings, not only by the authorities here, but utterly and entirely, by my home people, to whom I am simply unable to explain anything. I have no prospects of any material kind; I could not bear sustained mechanical work, and literature, to which I aspire, is too sacred. It is unnecessary for me to state that the 'poetry' I have perpetrated, since September, 1882, is enough to fill volumes. But I never feel that I can really *do* anything; poetry is being, is the projection of self into the wide spaces of unfilled imagination; I have no right to live by living; I believe in Carlyle, (whom do not misapprehend as anything else but a loving, tender fellow man, very earnest and suffering) and, believing in his words, refuse to be, to the external world, other than an inarticulate poet. I feel, as all must feel, who believe in spirituality, an intense love of beauty in all its forms: I realise to myself an infinity of love in listening to true music, in seeing true paintings, reading true poetry; but, in the midst of all this delight, I feel an impatient longing to crash discords into the music, to burn and destroy the poetry and painting with their memories, to be up and doing or suffering; the kind of state which goads men into the cloister or the gaming hell. Egoism, mere egoism, to waste your time in ravings: but I can't help it or myself. And nothing seems to give me any assistance; I try and find value in C. Kingsley, but find instead explanations of the Athanasian Creed; in Maurice, and he preaches of 'the eternal scheme of Redemption'.[1] I know that those

---

[1] Charles Kingsley (1819-75) was heavily influenced by Frederick Denison Maurice (1805-72), a co-founder of Christian Socialism and Professor at King's College, London. Johnson refers to Maurice's *Theological Essays* (1853), which so shocked the principal of King's with their 'dangerous doctrines' that he

who like myself feel this want of actuality, will have it supplied: I believe in the approach of a veritable Armageddon, an upheaval of the nations, wherein all true men must take their share as men and spirits. But I leave these matters, and turn elsewhere. I am rejoiced to hail in you a fellow Browningite: I adore Browning with an ecstasy well nigh passionate. I know that the feeling must appear extravagant, but I know also that it is sincere. Do make Russell love him; I know how infinitely he would find comfort in him, if only he would read him as he would an evangel of light.

I am agitating to found a literary society down here in the school; but we are very prosaic, and I meet with little response, but hope to effect something by articles in our papers.

If you write again, do not more than is essential, introduce Bhuddism as a topic: I know that such promises as I have made to my Father and the Masters here on the subject are mere evasions on both sides, but I am bound to respect them. I will certainly send you and Russell photos when I have them; at present I have not any.

Does it ever strike you that the nothingness of death is absolute? that, as there is no beginning of unknowable infinity, so there is no end to the boundless advance of time and time-caused change? Perhaps it is a truism, but it always strikes me when I think of it, as a newly revealed truth. I have been reading Comte and Mill together just now; such an absolute death in life as their respective philosophies I can scarcely realize: and then, the piteous certainty that they are

---

was summoned before the council and asked to resign.

both so hopelessly incapable of reaching the truth, whose beams are but behind the thin veil of materialism yet remaining. Comte's hierarchy of noble men is so grand a conception, but such a petrification of the truth that 'all things, yea, all men and holy angels, are fragments broken off from that high and central well of light, whose darting rays do by their streaming gold, commute the base things of earth into the liquid purity of most tender heaven'. A strange sentence, is it not? and, I venture to say, unknown to all the world but myself, being a MS remark I found in an old edition, unfortunately lost, of the *Pilgrim's Progress*.

I have now only to excuse myself for my Wintonian prolixity, and hope ever to be

Your afft friend,
L.P. Johnson

18

College
February 18, [1884]

Dear Sayle,

And is George Eliot's aspiration really the creed of mankind; does the 'choir invisible' really live only in 'memory of perfect deed'?[1] I do not want reason: I do not want argument: I want more light. Ah, I *know* the truth, I am inspired, I go about my daily trivialities with the words of the Most High on my closed lips

---

1 The opening lines in George Eliot, 'O May I Join the Choir Invisible!' (1867).

and in my heart, 'breaking for a little love':[1] I care nothing for all the vast seething darkness of the past life of aeons, or the white blankness of future light: I am in the present, and know all I *need*. In plainer words, apart from all manifestations of the infinite and unknowable in the creeds of church and school, I am an Idealist, Spiritualist, Transcendentalist. Yet, spite of the glory of intuition, the calm dignity of spiritual life is unknown to me: and sometimes I am ready to think that the spirit of light is the devil of orthodoxy, driving me down to the orthodox hell by the weapon of my self conceit. Ah, is Christ God? or is Fredric Harrison?[2] or am I truly the only God allowed to myself? I will accept any of them, if only I can live by him. But to one who, like myself, believes that he has the truth in inspiration, personal, uncommunicable truth, it is very hard to be unable to use it; to feel himself a 'temple of the Holy Ghost', yet see in himself no signs of sacrifice. Think for a moment of what we are: the awful mass of creed and nations and histories piled up behind us, and we, feeling ourselves urged on wildly by the force of inconceivable law into a future of haze and doubt. Suicide is a painfully logical act; were it not that I instinctively recoil from logic, I might grow afraid of it. I think you are right in what you say as to individuality: I can find in my art, if I may so call it, the most intense comfort. But I will talk on other topics awhile.

---

1 Christina Rossetti, 'L.E.L.' (1866).
2 Frederic Harrison (1831-1923), Positivist philosopher and historian.

I suppose you know Badley, at Rugby.[1] I wrote a few days ago at random to the Editor of the *Leaflet*, thinking that an expression of extraneous sympathy and appreciation might not be regarded as an intrusion: and I have received a most kind letter from him, recognizing my motives, deploring the lack of material and support at Rugby, and winding up by an appeal to me for contributions; so I have sent him a certain number of lyrics and short poems for him to do what he likes with any time.[2] The mysterious fascination of poetry is wonderful: to throw oneself out of oneself into one's inner self seems and is absolutely a passion with me.

You say that to know that I *am* here, ought to suffice me. But it does not suffice me; and how can it? if 'between two worlds life hovers like a star',[3] how can I guide my feeble flickerings, unless I know their origin and their true use? I know neither: only, 'that it is from God, to God'.[4] But that is not enough; my master Carlyle lived through eighty heroic years of inconceivable suffering, before he went to God: and his star was livid as a corpse-light, in ignorance of truth of spirit. You may say, that these powers unfold themselves; that I shall find my destined path the same as the one I take by chance. I think not: I think that when I am dying, without the rapturous hope of orthodoxy, of 'being

---

1 John Haden (Jack) Badley (1865-1967), the third recipient of the letters collected here.
2 Badley published the first of these in the next edition of *The Leaflet*, March 1884.
3 George Gordon, Lord Byron, *Don Juan* (1819-24), canto xv, stanza 99.
4 Romans 11:36: 'For of him, and through him, and to him, are all things'.

with Jesus'; without the firm faith of the East, of an earth-life ended; a period of probation over; without the trust of absolute extinction, which Schopenhauer would give me: without the high thought of a great example and worth to humanity, which George Eliot and Comte died with—without any of these, I shall leave the world, leave the earthly light, and depart, with one thought only: the thought of a life wasted. Here, however, I am not all destitute of hope: for the intuition of the spirit, the breath wafted from the land of dreams and shades, the faces of dead friends,—these I know are realities: I have a faith in the unseen, in the place of death. I will try to tell you a little of what I mean: you may understand. I have often gone into churchyards and even, when possible, vaults and charnel houses, to try to hear the truth from the lips of spirits, to force the paraphernalia of death to unfold their secret: I have tried, oh, so earnestly tried, in utter faith, to make the dead hear me, feel for me, comfort me. But the dead are deaf, or else too happy to listen. Don't think me mad: I am only human. You see, I *know* that there is a truth somewhere: I *will not accept it as a creed* of churches or philosophies: I will find it for myself out of myself: I believe in love as the key to unlock the spheres. Meanwhile, I must live a lonely life: life of art and patience: life of sympathy and self reliance: but, above all, a life of unseen relations, of spiritual (call them chimerical) visions and intuitions. I wld not waste my strength in solving questions of my own propounding: but the wind, the air, dreams, all bring me questions and keep on waiting for answers.

Ever yours,
L.P. Johnson

Don't think I am not giving yr letter enough thought: but I must write at once, before I lose my impressions.

Ridding's leaving is an inconsolable grief to me: he is the only person here who, (I am not speaking conceitedly), understands me at all.[1]

19

College
February 22, [1884]

Dearest Sayle,

I *do* know Shelley: and I know only too well 'the wide, grey, lampless, deep, unpeopled world'[2]—perhaps you know the rest; I think it is true. You say that I have not answered your letter: I say, you have not answered mine. I grant you that I cannot *attain to* my perfect ideal: I do not wish to do so: I want to find out its existence outside my imagination, and then aspire, aspire, 'immer und immer nach zu streben'.[3] I am afraid that what Russell says is true of me: I do not put my heart into my actions; I am selfish, towards those who are not objects of personal love on my part. Paracelsus failed, thro' want of love: I will fail with

---

[1] The Headmaster left Winchester to be consecrated first Bishop of Southwell on 1 May 1884.
[2] Percy Bysshe Shelley, *The Cenci* (1819), act v, scene iv.
[3] Always and always to strive. Quoted from memory from Goethe's *Faust* (part 1), 'Ihr nach und immer nach zu streben'.

him, rather than counterfeit God.[1] Do not think that I really have no love: I have too much to find a resting place for it, except in an ideal. I know how horrible this must sound—this indifference to my wretched brothers in this painfully real world, and this star- or God gazing into the infinite: but I must and can only repeat, I do feel these yearnings, and they are I; I can die, and find the truth: but I cannot kill them, and live; they are immortal, whilst I am a being.

Yes, there is good in every thing. I am too true a Browningite, and I know by heart 'Caliban upon Setebos' and much of 'Christmas Eve and Easter Day'.

You tell me to love; and to love 'humanity': what, I ask with Victor Hugo, is 'humanity'? I too am part of that abstraction; and I, *as human*, know my weakness, and will not be content to lean upon my brothers, to comfort them in return; pardon me, if I grieve you, but I say that 'humanity' is a sham, a mass of suffering; and you bid us exchange each other's loves, and be content.

Who gave me my longings? God, I mean, the Unknowable, knows they are not of my seeking; I find them in me, as did Plato; but I do not argue back with him and Wordsworth: I prophesy forward into the future. Do not ask me to be logical, to dispute points, to answer you: 'Video meliora, proboque: Deteriora sequor':[2] there is my answer, as you would put it into my mouth: not that I see better things; I see realities, and follow shadows. I, as Beddoes, says, 'with

---

1 Robert Browning, *Paracelsus* (1835).
2 Ovid, *Metamorphoses*, vii. 21: I see the better way and approve, but follow the worse way.

half my soul inhabit other worlds'.¹ By nature, I am painfully exclusive, and unprepossessing: I feel myself born too late: I ought to have been an Alchemist, and have searched, alone, for the Elixir of Life, and died, on the brink of finding it.

Ah, is not all life a looking for the Elixir? then perhaps Death is the well of life? then I can look forward for Death. Is not the world a real thing: I mean, real in essence? then there must be its counterpart in man: I see the leaves rotting in autumn: I see my friends die: I see spring come: I feel my friends live still. That is my nearest approach to a formula. You do but take upon you the executioner's disguise which Schopenhauer invented, and scent it free with perfumes from the taint of blood, and put the blossom of love in its button hole, and ask me to wear it. I will not: I appeal to Schopenhauer's two tests or images—Nature, Music. When I see the world, 'the sun, the moon, the stars, the seas, the hills, and the plains',² I see life, dying and quickened, ever changing, and growing up, species evolved from species, air and light and growth. When I listen, as I am listening as I write, to the glorious notes of an organ, I hear what Abt Vogler heard: a pledge of immortality. I find no death in life. I turn to man, and have hope: but not certainty. I find in this an evident truth: all being for the best, certainty

---

1 Thomas Lovell Beddoes, *Lines Written in Switzerland* (1851) quoted from memory: 'But if there be, who, having laid the loved / Where they may drop a tear in roses' cups, / With half their hearts inhabit other worlds'.

2 Tennyson, 'The Higher Pantheism' (1867): 'The sun, the moon, the stars, the hills and the plains—/ Are not these, O Soul, the Visions of Him who reigns!'

is undesirable; then, I must have faith. But faith, to be faith, cannot rest in itself: so, with you I will love, or try to love: with my own spirit, I will aspire, away, far away, and find out the author of my faith. And, ah, you tell me that I am but looking for myself!

Don't misunderstand me: I will not write a Gospel, or be even as Swedenborg, or write an autobiography of my Spirit: I will, despite love trying to shelter materialism, I will aspire to the Unseen.

My companions here, would say, 'Moonshine': you say, 'you are seeking a Will o'the Wisp.' Well, I am: I confess it: I am crying for the moon, and I am stumbling thro' marshes after a Will o'the Wisp: but, are not Moons and Wisps realities? they elude us, or placidly look down upon us, but they exist, and bid us seek them; I do but obey their call, I do not invent it.

I am only repeating myself: I will try to formulate my letter: 'I am willing to grant that you are right, in all but one point: i.e., that I am of my own will seeking shadows: I am called to follow them and cannot stop by the way to be a good Samaritan.'

I can say nothing but just that: call me insensible, inhuman, self-deluded: I will not defend myself.

I know that the gods of ages have gone away: I know that change is the condition of existence: I do not know that the heavens are empty spaces, save for the Light of Love. I fill them up with spirits.

I have not heard from my father just lately: but I thank you, tho' I know the result.[1] He cannot under-

---

[1] Sayle had written to Captain Johnson at Russell's instigation asking him to rescind the ban on his son's correspondence with

stand what I feel, and I cannot explain and dissect my soul.

I can not—no, I can, but am too tired,—write any more.

Thank Russell: I know what he is feeling about me. I may be too scrupulous, but I had rather not hear from him, as long as I have pledged myself to solitude.[1]

With thanks and melancholy,
Ever yours,
L.P. Johnson

23rd.

I did not send this yesterday, so add a few words.

If you really wish in any way to assist me, explain to me how your gospel differs from a refined and,— permit the paradox,—loving Stoicism. You will not look forward or back; you simply do your obvious duty, and love your brothers: very well, but is that all? you must feel that you cannot exist in uncertainty: at least, I cannot understand your enduring it. I cannot understand George Eliot's life, as you seem to do. Read, if you can, Howells' *Undiscovered Country*[2] and, in Myers' *Essays, Modern*, the confessions of faith of George Sand and Mazzini, especially the latter. Vale!

Russell. Russell described Captain Johnson's reply of 24 Feb 1884 as 'kind but hopeless'.
1 Letter 16 had so upset Russell that he wrote a letter to Johnson and threatened to send it, despite the ban.
2 William Dean Howells, *The Undiscovered Country* (1880).

20

College
March 1, [1884]

Dear Sayle,

I am, at this moment, radiantly happy at the discovery of a new form of verse, a virtuoso bliss which is to me exquisite: so I take opportunity to write.

I have nothing to tell you: the sun is bright and, which is better, warm: the sky is blue and a bird is twittering somewhere. I feel as happy as I can allow myself to be. Also, I have just read Fred: Harrison's 'Ghost of Religion' in the *Nineteenth Century*: it completely squashes the vapid Agnostic and the vague Churchman; and gives us 'Humanity' as the only genuine article; well, there I part company, and ally myself with the primeval savage who 'deduced God from ghosts'; but I won't dispute anything with anybody.

Strange, what a difference a glorious day can make! how one revels in life, in being, in poetry, in the holy ridiculousness of things! As to your and Russell's coming down here—I am awkwardly situated.[1] As to you, I have no hesitation: to the eyes of authority, you are a harmless person, and a friend of mine: but Russell is a 'bête noire', and the people here would expect us to preach or hold meetings or something; seriously, I don't know about him: morally, of course he can come: but practically, I am uncertain. Yes! you shall

---

1 Having failed to convince Johnson's father to end the ban on their correspondence, Russell asked Sayle to appeal to Johnson directly for permission to visit him at Winchester. The visit took place 5-7 Apr 1884.

come, both of you! it is absurd to suppose that two respectable individuals are to be debarred from going about by the quakings of orthodox conscience. But, if it wld suit you, come earlier: the Sixth, by some blessed arrangement, have no exams:, to speak of, this half, so that by Thursday, at least, I should be absolutely dying of ennui, which is the worst death. I am glad my Father answered you: I can imagine what he said: very earnest, but, if I may say so, wrong headed.

What are you going to do 'in life'? I have no prospects material or otherwise: perhaps literature will swallow me up, as many scribblers before. I *do* hate, as Russell hates, scholarship, in the technical sense. I won't be a pedant, and I won't learn philology or occupy myself with 'theories of the midelle verb' [*sic*]. I love classic literature, and scholarship so far as it elucidates that, but I am not in the world to dissect or vivisect. Which word, as I am in a discursive mood, reminds me of a question, which answer: do you hate and abhor vivisection, even under anaesthetics, as the incarnate manifestation of atheism and uncleanness? you must, but I know Russell is a heretic: convert him.

So you have renounced chapel services: I cannot sympathise: I love all services, from Roman Catholic down to Little Bethel:[1] they are like reading poetry in their effects of laughter and tears. In any case, I never feel a repugnance. 'What's the best thing in the world? Some thing out of it, I think.' Mrs: Browning's words are my creed: but how I get the 'something' into the world? I can get myself out, but I can't take

---

1 Nonconformist chapel in Charles Dickens, *The Old Curiosity Shop* (1841).

my brothers: your Humanity steps in: we are not opposed, really.

I suppose you find that you vary with the weather? I mean, your creed has a kind of barometer, as the influences change. Just now, I feel all love; so I am going to walk away down the river this afternoon, and read Emerson: my idea of love finding partial expression. Yes, do come, both, and don't hesitate: you see, my father could not object to that: he is too rational.

Oh, life is so good, and men are so wretched! and I am so happy because of the sunshine! there is a logical connection. Vale! No, Χαίρε![1]

Ever yours,
L.P. Johnson

Excuse writing: I hope you are getting used to it: anyhow it may act as a thorn in the flesh.

21

College
March 22, [1884]

Dear Sayle,

On going out of doors this morning for the first time for a week, having been in bed with abominable influenza, I was comforted by two good things—your handwriting and a glorious spring day: I read the one whilst walking far away in the other: as to prayer and

---

[1] Chairē. Both Vale and Chairē can be translated as 'farewell', but the former has the implication of wishing one strength and health, while the latter implies a wish for delight and joy.

worship—well, I did both whenever I looked about me: I mean, the feeling of joy and hope and (pardon the expression) immortality, is prayer: for as I did not give myself these glories of nature, nor deserve them, I must be grateful: whether to the daisies and primroses, or a reflex of myself in Heaven, I neither know nor care: I don't worship God: I worship myself, sometimes: and always I worship looking back. I am not lucid just now, but I may be intelligible. As to Winchester—Saturday would be in every way suitable for every one, if, as you say, it suits you: if this weather holds out, the place ought to look like a Paradise: but I always idealise places I love so intensely as I do Winchester.

Poor Badley! I know, I told him, I shld be illegible: but it doesn't matter, to him, or me either, except in the matter of personal correspondence. Why will you run down Rugby so unfilially? it can't be more Philistian than this place is—and it is not obscure tho' it is midland, which you seem to regard as a crime. I couldn't start periodicals in a literary way here: we are all very materialistic and social and political, and wld rather ape the Spectator with a flavour of the World. To my disgust, advantage was taken of my illness to elect me Literary Editor of the productions of the Shakespeare Society, in company with Cruickshank, Billson, and Hardy, all of New:[1] it means endless correspondence, and printers suicidal.

[1] Alfred Hamilton Cruickshank (1862-1927) and Henry John Hardy (1860-1939) were both at New College and both became assistant masters at Winchester; Charles James Billson (1857-1932) was at Christ Church and afterwards became a solicitor, writer and translator.

It is not irrational to pray; don't you see that we are very weak, and circumstances very strong, and no communication between the two? ergo, pray: not that your prayer is 'heard' by any one or thing: but it is a comfort, just as music is: I almost think true lives impossible, without a kind of ceremonial creed: I agree with Newton Hall there.[1]

No more time.

Ever yours,
L.P. Johnson

'Excuse weak thoughts!' but I am not exactly flourishing.

22

King's Mead, Windsor Forest
[13 or 20 April, 1884][2]

Dear Sayle,

I got your absurd letter this morning, and write a few lines in answer. First of all, my thanks for your roses, which I spiritually devoured. Next, as to your visit. I know perfectly that I myself was unable to appreciate it as I might have, thro' my deafness:[3] but as to its being an intrusion—well, that's nonsense entirely.

Why did I go to Church this morning to listen to

---

1 The home of Frederic Harrison's splinter group of Positivists.
2 Though correctly sequenced, this letter was incorrectly dated 27 March by Russell. Reference to Sayle's recent visit to Winchester on 7 April (Russell's diary) and Ridding's departure more accurately date it as either Sunday 13 or 20 April.
3 Presumably a sequela to Johnson's influenza the previous month.

dirgelike Litanies with intervals for meditation? why didn't I go into the fields and enjoy the primroses and spring? and why is Jesus' death insisted on and his life ignored? Ah well! it is all mournfully amusing, and amusement is a holy thing. I hardly know what is the reason of my absurd delight in theology, so called: just now I am absorbing *Tracts for the Times*, most attractive in many ways. It seems so strange, that we know nothing of death, and everything about eternity.

I made an era in my life in saying good-bye to Dr. Ridding on Tuesday: I feel so by myself now, and with such a strange sensation of superiority and conceit! isn't it so?

What is sin, in itself? I want you to give me a definition of your idea of it.

I envy you Trin: Coll: Cambridge: it is exactly what Coleridge called architecture—'frozen music'.[1]

With regard to myself, it is a satisfaction to me to know that I shall not be deaf all my life: tho' I often wish I could be deaf and blind, and live inwardly.

I write in haste, and disconnectedly: pardon it.

Yrs,

L. Johnson.

P.S. I have got your other lost letter from Wolverhampton!

The line you ask about is an original hexameter of Shelley's written by him and signed in a visitor's book

---

1 The statement 'Music is liquid architecture; Architecture is frozen music' is usually attributed to Goethe. Sayle is at home in Cambridge for the holidays.

in an inn in the Alps: underneath some Christian has written, 'The fool hath said &c.':[1] on wh: Swinburne remarks, 'What 'the fool' did write, the reader can judge.' The line says little for Shelley's scholarship in point of spelling.

L.P.J.

23

King's Mead, Windsor Forest
April 26, [1884]

Dear Sayle,

So the world has given its verdict at last: the respectable, intelligent, appreciative world? Well, I am so heartily glad.[2] But I will give you the best account of myself that I can. I will begin with two statements: I am a Browningite: I love the beautiful Quaker doctrine, 'Love the sinner and condemn (hardly that: depends on case)[3] the sin': you must assimilate these two things as real, active facts. Then, I do truly and earnestly believe that at the end, all is right. I find myself in the world: I am confronted with thoughts, fashions, ways of life, fellow men: whereas all I want is, to live my own life. You can scarcely understand how intensely I live alone: how alien and strange and laughable everything appears to me but myself. As a child, I found one of my chief pleasures in secretly

---

1 Psalm 14:1: 'The fool hath said in his heart, There is no God'.
2 This letter refers to rumour of Johnson's 'immoral behaviour' as described in the Introduction.
3 This comment added as an afterthought.

pulling to pieces the Bible, in unconsciously noticing every thing about me with a kind of precociously artistic manner, as if I were a dramatist: the latter trait I retain.

I have been told by people who have been my friends that I am naturally, by birth, devoid of so called conscience and moral instinct: I never really know when I am absolutely sincere in thought: but in tastes and actions I am perfectly consistent and sincere. Accordingly, I live my own life, and not some other life.

I once in an essay for Ridding defined happiness as 'the having full scope in one's own sphere and circle for practicing that rule of life which practice and instinct have approved.' Ridding looked at me with a smile, and said: 'you have come into the world too late for that.' He stated appreciatively the case as it is. My happiness is of my own making: as I have told you, I love music, I love flowers, I love literature, I love studying people: except in matters of taste, i.e., matters of culture, no one can excite my loathing nor my indignation. After reading Thomas à Kempis, I can listen with no disgust to sensual conversation:[1] I can return freely to walk over the downs. As I love the simple nobility of the literature, the beautiful world of nature, so I can take pleasure in the thoughts and minds of other natures. Don't misunderstand me: I have not the pen of Browning to make a gulf of dif-

---

1 Most likely Johnson refers to *Of the Imitation of Christ* and the lines, 'Whatever a man cannot amend either in himself or in others he ought to bear patiently, until God orders things otherwise'.

ference appear between shades of meaning. I do not love sensuality: I do not hate it: I do not love purity: I do not hate it: I regard both as artistic aspects of life. 'But,' you will say, 'in real earnest life, you must take a side.' True: and I ask myself how I ought to walk: I am answered, in the words of a poetess, 'Where thy own footsteps would be leading.'[1] When I am in town, they lead to the National Gallery and the Albert Hall: when in my own room, to turning poetaster: when I meet with a question of morals, to the question, not 'What does my conscience tell me I should do', but, 'By doing what, would your artistic instinct be satisfied? What does the moment tell you it requires for itself?' Show all this rhapsody to Northcote,[2] and he will say it's all nonsense, I am a sham, I am simply immoral, and don't like confessing it in words, so veil it with words. I know I have lost many friends by my life: I may be about to lose more: but, (don't be disgusted) their very losses are to me no more than incidents, from which to derive artistic pleasure: don't think me a heartless dilettante, if I tell you that all this episode is to be intensely delightful: that I left off a quasi Browningite versification of it, to write to you. It is not that I am insincere now: I know my thoughts shift, but that is inevitable: my actions are true and sincere. I will, notwithstanding, come to details.

'I ought to have left the school.'

Required, an answer.

---

[1] Emily Brontë, 'Stanzas' (1850): 'I'll walk where my own nature would be leading: / It vexes me to choose another guide'.
[2] George Russell Northcote (1863-1920) was perhaps the perpetrator of the rumour.

I ought not.

My way of life, which I will never renounce, naturally, logically, brings me very near to infringement of the world's, especially the school-world's, ten commandments. As a prefect, I will not take steps in the matter of 'immorality': as a junior, I never shrunk back from any society: I do not *now*. I will not call any thing 'sin': I deal neither in 'poison nor pap':[1] I am an 'impressionist' in life. I openly told Ridding last half, in almost these words, my convictions—no, God's convictions in me: and he did understand me, in a way most lovingly gentle and sympathetic: he told me he did not expect me to be able to do two things: to keep myself (from my own point of view) unspotted from the world; and to have any friends in the world. The latter is quite true, painfully true sometimes: but the first I deny. In spite of all my mental state during the past year, I return to my oldest station: I cannot violate my own nature. Asceticism is wrong, as a rule of life, sensuality is wrong, as a disorder of life: but asceticism is right when the moment cries out with Faust, 'Entbehren sollst du':[2] and sensuality, when it whispers, 'eat and drink, for tomorrow we die'.

Ah yes, I know what you must think of all this: how at variance you must think it with high nobility, with aspiration, with the respectability of the British nation: I can't say more plainly what I think.

---

1 An echo of Algernon Charles Swinburne's 1866 reply to accusations of sensuality, immorality and blasphemy in his *Poems and Ballads*: 'We, meanwhile, who profess to deal neither in poison nor in pap, may not unwillingly stand aside. Let those read who will, and let those who will abstain from reading'.
2 You must abstain (*Faust*, part 1).

You want to refute what you hear? but you can't refute truth as the world gives it you: at best you may say to the world, 'you say, quite correctly, that two and two make four: and I am afraid it is true that my friend (?) makes them make five: but he has got a monomania, was born so: it's all very sad!' Forgive me, if I offend your feelings: I must, if you want me to defend my own.

Perhaps you take up Jesus' attitude: 'no one has a right to condemn you, but still you are damnable in the abstract: therefore, sin no more!' I have explained my answer to that.

Dear Sayle, if you really cannot accept this, if you think I am a sham, at least it may be some comfort to you to know that no event in life can wound me: I am invulnerable. Do you know Walt Whitman?

'Blessed are the pure in heart, for they see God.'[1]

Can you evoke from my 'apologia pro vitâ meâ' that I see God?

Again, forgive me for possible injuries and *believe* me,

Yrs affectionately,
Lionel Johnson

Show this to any one you like: I am indifferent, either way.

---

1 Matthew 8:5.

24

King's Mead, Windsor Forest
April 30, [1884]

Dear Sayle,

Thanks for your letter and its enclosure, which I return without having really had time to study it. My rough, crude impression is, that its author was a poetical thinker, not a thinking poet. I mean, his thoughts, true and very beautiful, occasionally suffer from monotony of presentment: without being a plagiarist or otherwise than original, he might, I think, have infused a little more mannerism into his verse, viewed as an art-product: but I can sincerely admire it from many points of view to me less important.

Do I know Beddoes? and do I know Thomson? the questions seem so strange. Beddoes' is an instance of simple Art without the necessary foundation of natural instinct: his *Death's Jest Book* is a wonderful poem, but such a wonderful copy of old models! but he is one of my favourites, tho' I have never been able to get hold of any of his works permanently.

Thomson I hear much of, since I knew a friend of his: and I have the story of his life; and love him for it. A poem which George Eliot loved is certainly noteworthy: but in this case the love is deserved: I never saw elsewhere such artistic pessimism.[1]

By the way, who is the author of your lines? he has absorbed too much Shelley to be good for his poetry.

---

1 The poem Eliot admired was James B. V. Thomson's *The City of Dreadful Night* (1874).

I know many Nichols' by name, and can't distinguish yours or his book, tho' I know its name.

I go to town tomorrow for Ridding's 'consecration': as if he wanted it!

Convocation has almost relieved itself from the stigma of the Horton business by its note of yesterday: another good gift from the hands of High Churchmen.[1]

I have no time just now, a fact my writing will tell you.

Ever yours,
L. Johnson

25

College
May 4, [1884]

Dear Sayle,

I scarcely understand you, as a whole. I see quite distinctly and with clear insight the tendency of your last letter, but now [sic] the mind that directed it. You want, you will have, definitions of definitions: you say, do I recognize a morality, &c? and, of course, as real things? Yes, they are real things to me: I maintain that I am (how I loathe the word!) 'moral': moral in act and thought. But that is only my opinion.

---

[1] Convocation (the Governing Body of the University of Oxford) had decided to allow women to sit some honours examinations at Oxford, as compared with their former rejection of Nonconformist New College fellow Robert Forman Horton (1855-1934) as an examiner.

The beautiful Church of Rome, which I love and honour beyond all other institutions for God-manufacture, has strange morality: a priest told me last week that 'the divine Christ should have been a sinner: how else can God love, how else be God, unless by pardoning sin as an act of infinite logic?'

Do I acknowledge right and wrong? Oh no, how can I? am I eternal? I strive and struggle against ugliness, against the frightful pruriency which fills our streets with lost (!) women and our society with graceful debauchees: and I know neither wrong nor right, but I know that ugliness is the end of some things and beauty and the beauty of holiness of others: don't you know the last lines of Browning's 'Statue and the Bust'?

Is morality of any value? yes, marketable and otherwise: it has saved souls and burned bodies; loved and hated, run the round of antithesis. In daily life, it means, I think, reduced to common sense, the combination of courtesy and self-respect. Small things, you think: not high and noble.

Byron and Shelley: Rome and Athens: wrong and right: I care more for your words on these men than any others of yours. Shelley's 'spirituality'! and Byron's passionate 'sensualism'!

Did you ever read the *Revolt of Islam*? have you studied Shelley's life? do you know his letters? how does he define morality?

The truth is, that nothing is common or unclean: there is no sin and no devil.

Sensuality: what is it, unless the expression of the *mind* instead of the *spirit*? such a thing as the *Excursion* is to the 'Ode on Duty'?[1] limelight instead of the stars? it leads to ruin of body and grossness of spirit: alas, yes! but not till Morality has spurned it and trampled on it.

Do you know anything of Blake and his gospel? if you really want to know my meaning, turn to him. I do not pretend to have found a new gospel: I am only Christian enough and conceited enough at the age of seventeen to assert that I can assist the cause of the world by the gospel of universal love and pardon: I could kneel at the feet of all the 'sins' and ask their blessing: because I do not know why and wherefore I should condemn them. Do not isolate parts of conduct: don't say, 'This man has been a thief, that man is honest: I will give tracts to the one and my blessing to the other': for, you see, you don't know very much outside yourself.

My enthusiasm is as true as any man's: Humanity is a sham: but poor sinning men and women are no shams, and I will not condemn them or their sins: how do I know? I do love the cause of Love and Charity: the world does not.

Oh, think what a human soul is: think how it works within itself and is but itself, whilst you are quite other than it! personify sin if you will: you can't include all in the capital letter.

Milton perforce made the devil his hero.

I picture frame, it is true: but whereas some pictures are things to shudder at for their unspiritual imbecility of origin, others are not so: and I can judge

---

1 Poems by William Wordsworth (1814 and 1807 respectively).

accordingly: only, in the soul, all pictures are God's work. 'Logic and sermons never convince: am I inconsistent? very well, I am inconsistent.'[1]

>With which quotation,
>Yours wonderingly,
>L. Johnson

---

1 Walt Whitman, 'Song of Myself' in *Leaves of Grass* (1855).

PART 2
I AM A PRIEST!

26

Read this first.[1]

College
May 10, [1884]

Dearest Sayle,

In this beautiful spring, where life is so beautiful and the world so mystical, I can think more clearly than at other times: and now I have been told by the inspiration of the spring what is best for my life as a man.

I can only bore you with all this: but I can not help that.

My conclusions may surprise you: I will be a priest, of the Church of England, as I have so often dreamed of being. I will explain: I do long with all my energies of hope to be an influence: I have the wish undefined. My nature can only lead me to the methods of spiritual, artistic, emotional expression; and I feel that for this to be carried out I must have

---

1 Sent to Sayle with letter 27.

ground to stand upon. For, you know, we do believe all that Christianity gives us: and time and the spirit of historic impulse have moulded Christianity into many forms for influencing man: and I now see plainly that in all things, religion and science, state policy and soup kitchens, organization is imperative. I do not, perhaps, believe that Jesus is a personal God: but I believe in Jesus: he may be dead: but not his words on life; they are deathless. I can conscientiously (oh, that pestilential word!) 'take orders': I love the expression. What hypocrisy is there in enrolling myself with the visible spiritualists; shall I turn my poor back on the Church because it is a medley of grotesque and divine? I may try and write something not all unworthy of being read: but that is not work altogether, and I distrust myself. I cannot bear to think of the Church simply left to drift itself hopelessly into vacuity, for the want of fresh steersmen: it is a live protest against materialism, and shall not die. A body which has embraced Keble, Mansel, Stanley, Maurice, Robertson, Pusey, etc. can surely tolerate even me? and I am not certain how far I am justified in refusing to join the Church, so long as nothing from myself tells me no: if the Church cast me off, well, I can let go: but not till then. Only think of the chances which the priesthood offers: the countless influences of the pulpit and altar, all potent against the devil in even feeble hands: and how I could train myself! All other ways of communion with the spirits of our brothers are so half hearted: altruism from the independent standpoint of misty intuition unsupported by circumstances may be noble in the abstract: but have all the cliques and sets of philosophers won the world? I know the Society of Jesus and the Brotherhood of St. Francis of Assisi as mighty influences: hardly the Positivists and Idealists. Don't misunderstand me: I acknowledge the higher view of solitary truth, regarded as not solitary but only *the truth* in an uncongenial soil: but you will never make the soil congenial by preaching noble uncongenialities! I, with labour, might do a little work for you as a pioneer.

I feel more encouraged by what I have told you lately: I have such perfect sympathy with all forms of life and thought, and nothing really is repulsive to me: I do think I might do good. All truth is one: some truth wears strange garments.

By the way, I protest against your pithy denunciation of 'aestheticism': in the vulgar sense, I mostly agree with you: but so far as it means the gospel of emotion waking as an artistic morality, it is a high hope for mankind: true, never lotus eat: lotus is poison, and, in truth, an insidious and unknown one. Write soon—

Yrs ever
L. Johnson

I did think of the Church of Rome: I am not sure yet! but you see what I am driving at.

27

College
May 13, [1884]

Dear Sayle,

I send you a double instalment of epistolary boredom: the first I forgot to post.

I have just got your letter: thank you.

So people still 'defame'? pardon me, I do not know 'that beast of a word, defame'. Oh, the world does: but then, that poor world of impossible grotesques! I write in front of a mass of marsh flowers of kinds, and laugh at the world, and love it.

Someone is now trying to make the organ tell me that 'I know that my redeemer liveth!' It does it very lamely, but that is inevitable: my flowers tell it me plainly, tho' you seem to doubt it.

Will you pardon me, if I say that to me you appear too—don't laugh!—too 'serious'; not, of course, in a true sense of the word, but you seem to me hardly to appreciate the happiness of circumstances. I stated my 'artistic' views the other day to you, and you were indignant; I now soften them. Can not you laugh at and with, everything? death, Christ, yourself, your friends, your fears, your life, your hopes....? I do, invariably: and I am not irreverent. I simply feel that life is exquisitely humorous, even in its miseries: and my laughter brightens it. Ah, life is very awful, with its infinitudes of woe and doubt: then don't think about all these things as sorrows, but as questions and jests of an unknown God, which he wants us to guess at and laugh over. A bad painting: a starving family: a false note: all wrong, equally wrong, all springing from the same causes, all to be remedied, protested against. Love: love everyone, and all things: Laugh at bad things, and, as an American mystic says, 'kiss them white'.

I have just had a new experience: I have completely lost my temper. I have received an omen: viz, the discovery that I have inadvertently torn up my first 'serious' attempt at tragedy: (my earliest was at the age of eight, and began in Purgatory). Of the ruins I only discovered a few lines which I inflict upon you, they being very ominous in their preservation.

But I can laugh, I think, now.

Such Godly weather! oh, such getting up early to see the sun rise, and watching the beautiful moon by night! that poor world: I hope it is happy. I am.

If I seem somewhat French and disconnected, it is because I have been swallowing Victor Hugo, a large supper for the Gods: but such a God himself! and so gentle.

Fearon is very 'nice': as yet, no more or less.[1]

I think Buddhism is not an approachable subject: but then, it is not Buddhism, it is the world! if that is not casuistry.

A priest! I am to be a priest! What do you think of it? do think of it, as I put it in my first letter: I am almost decided.

Of course, I don't mean a mitre in a shrine, or even a stall: but a vantage ground of my own, an enticing people under the pretence of shovel hattism, to put it openly. Oh, it is a high ideal!

---

1 William Andrewes Fearon (1841-1924) took over from Ridding as Headmaster of Winchester College.

Reflect: for what else am I suited? literature does not teach people as I want to teach them (allow the conceit): and I won't degrade it, as people say. Reflect.

I have carefully studied the Prayer Book, and the priest making part: I can honourably go thro' that process.

Knox Little[1] is going to preach here some time: could you come and hear him again?

Possibly I shall be at New College by October year: otherwise, two years: I want the latter, my people, the former: I love this home so very much.

I must conclude—

Yours affly,
L. Johnson

'Beyond all strain of aching human eyes
The expectation of white angels is,
And pleasant garden walls for washen souls.
Have you not seen where, in a western tract,
The sun shoots clear, green tapers up to God,
Athwart a bed of spreading primroses?
I think you cannot see the ends of them
Cling in soft network at the feet of God,
But your sight fadeth into pearly haze,
Or, caught aside by a first peeping star,
Hangs on the troubled bosom of the day.
I think you cannot see beyond these things,
Not tho' your eyes should catch the falling dews,
Nightly, and the grey owls should be to you
As dear, familiar friends, from long aspect
Of the same cloudy moon.'

---

[1] William John Knox-Little (1839-1918), High-Church Anglican cleric.

There: that is the only relic of my 'tragedy'! What an omen!

The speaker was a melancholy middle-aged modern man: speaking to a girl.

28

College
May 19, [1884]

Dearest Sayle,

Last night I sat up in the moonlight from eleven to four, with a very clever and strange quasi-friend of mine, discussing theories, especially mine: and now I get your letter. Altogether, I am provided with thought. I will make one remark to stand good for the future: as a personal favour, don't talk to me of Positivism. I won't have Materialism, the only -ism I can't love: and Positivism by its accursedly presumptuous name condemns itself.

No! I have not found my God, in your sense: for I never lost him; never doubted him: by 'him' I mean, facts and thoughts and persons and possibilities, not I, but part of me. That God is in the Church, is he not, as well as any otherwhere? Oh yes! I could be a Baptist, a Romanist, an Anglican, a Mormon, with almost equal faith.

Don't think I have no convictions capable of accurate definition: I have, on many points: but I hate definition, as a meanness towards the Infinite.

You are not 'aequo animo'[1] with regard to bishops and lawn sleeves and that ilk: of course there is nothing in them of holy: but is a government official with a taste for red tape cause for eschewing the constitution? I will be—no! am now—a priest, because I take the priesthood for my office in the world. One man paints, writes, fights, diplomatizes, loves, &c: I am a priest. And truly so: for my own nature leads me thither ward, almost to Ultramontanism. I am not changed: I am hardly inconsistent. Prayers for all and sundry, grotesque and arabesque in creed,—well, what of that? is that the Church's raison d'etre or stand point?

To come to details—I am, prospectively, a consecrated priest: I am set apart: well! the world can't get over the fact, and it likes it: the world even listens complacently: it is a little roused: I may do some good: I won't have a parish, but try and get the loaves and fishes by literature. I will be all things to a few men. Conceited? no! only the priestly element in strong assertion.

You hardly go—pardon me—deep enough into the creeds: you, I imagine, find no stumbling block to your admiration of Athens, in the fact that it believed in Olympus Gods: nay, they transfigured sea and land: but the Trinity? you say. Well, so the Trinity, as an intellectual aspiration.

I have a very firm faith in the hierarchy as a need of humanity: I think man is made for priests.

So, the Bhuddist system does not in that way disgust me, but rather elevates me.

---
1 Of even mind.

For the last two or three years I have worn round my neck out of sight a Rosary, blessed by Pius IX, given me by a dying Romanist cousin, whose last words were, 'you will use it in Paradise, if not before that'. I know as no one else can, the value of such 'superstition'.

How can I laugh? oh, how could I not do so! Do you not see, that the only true way of religious life is a profound irreverence, so to speak? a kind of jesting with God, or universal merriment? 'I am a priest: I am also a man, who love and laugh! I tell you as God's truth that the mystery of pain is merely the mark of joy, that all things are full of joy and audacious revelry: that Artemus Ward[1] and Thomas à Kempis are brothers; I am a priest.'

Do you understand? If you possess a dictionary, strike out of it the words 'materialism' and 'rationalize'. They are Satan and Beelzebub. You rationalize the Church! Why, the Church is spiritual, and your spirit must feel her spirit! Christ is up to date, beyond it: but a dead man. His spirit lives, and is alive for ever more: Amen. *Thus* is Christ risen from the dead: thus, his visible spirit ascended up to God, seen of his disciples, the likeness of a man, of a man, being God by light of manhood glorified. Is that orthodox? or only the Truth? I don't care. All the world over, you get the unloveliness of bishops &c: but roses have thorns, even in Paradise.

'Mutual forgiveness of each vice,
Such are the gates of Paradise.'

---

[1] Pen name of Charles Farrar Browne (1834-67), American comic writer and performer.

I am of Blake's humanity: do, please, read him, if you can.

Poor Northcote! how very miserable he ought to be! and how foolish of him. Well, he is food for laughter, so he has a mission.[1]

How do flowers tell me my Redeemer lives? because I see in them Paley's 'evidence of design' i.e., incarnate love. What right have flowers to be beautiful, unless they are full of love and real divinity? Flowers have souls. I don't mean this poetically but really as a spiritual syllogism. And don't think I am a dilettante jester: I know how uncouth the world is to a great extent, and long to do good: so I say: 'There is no hell: no sin: no anthropomorphism: no evil: no uncleanness: all love: no philosophy except of the spirit: I am a priest.'

Just grasp the attitude as you would a Browning study: you must see it.

Oh why has the Church failed, but because it talks of sin and not love? let me try my best.

Do you know 'Saul'?[2] or believe in it? Christ, the one completion of humanity, being the most human in his divinity? and, observe, Christ is a pure man, all man, essential man: full of warm life and love, a perfect man: but, all God, the thought! raised to the glories of ecstatic passion of love and the Godhead by the force of the surging fire of love: God in essence, man in substance, perfect God, perfect man!

---

1 What Northcote had done to deserve this comment is unknown unless he was indeed the perpetrator of the rumours about Johnson.
2 By Robert Browning (1855).

Is that orthodox? or only true? I think I am no heretic. The Church is a holy thing: full of error and whitewash and dead men's bones and potential love! Perhaps I may make my laughter clearer to you, by the force of love: I mean, love precludes sorrow except the passion of regret or aspiration; never wailing. Do animals not feel for their bereavements? yet they are silent but for the eyes.

Love! incarnate love of man for man, becoming God! God and man, all one, divinity paradoxical.

Ave, Maria, ora pro nobis!

There! is not that a real act of love: that wild, gentle cry to the incarnate maidenhood of the ideal love, ora pro nobis! Not we ourselves, not we, but thou, be thou us to God!

Oh Sayle, I think you can be a priest yet.

'Earth's Immortalities'![1] What! are the 'memory, hope, love of vanished years', all that is ours?[2] no! I know nothing, I am ignorant, only a priest of God! but love is God and when we love we are creators of God, the new creation of starfire and immortal tears! Oh God! thy priest, thy priest!

Yours ever,
Lionel

Comment vous appelez-vous?[3] please burn this: don't ask me why: at least, the second sheet.[4]

---

1 Also by Robert Browning (1845).
2 Christina Rossetti, 'Echo' (1862) quoted from memory: 'O memory, hope, love of finished years.'
3 What do you call yourself?
4 The second sheet (assuming that it was not burnt) extends from 'To come to details' to 'Artemus Ward and Thomas à Kempis are

I have no photo: am glad thereof: can you guess why?

29

College
May 24, [1884]

Dearest Sayle,

I hope I shall have heard from you before you get this: I don't know why I write: and I ought to be reading Guizot.

Perhaps it is because I have been reading again the *City of Dreadful Night*: good God, it is dreadful! but see what poor Thomson makes of your humanizing Love: how impotent it is by itself!

And what do I place with it? what twin divinity of emotion? Well, I hardly can formulate shadows: say, the meaning of the Trinity, the significance of Science, the 'mystery of pain'. Words! words! all phantoms of my ignorance, mere prating visions of the Invisible. But—a pulpit! and the Divine, the Beautiful, the Incarnate Abstract, the Imminent Concrete! Oh, to beguile men's minds with these, to juggle with my false position as a violin player with his God: raising and depressing emotions by the art of impulse! Is this horrible? search and see.

I am very restless: can never be at work in a groove: but I am faithful to the Spirit Land! I think you hardly realise the intense reality to some minds of the

---

brothers; I am a priest'.

Spirits: how they rustle their wings against our dusty, sin flushed, sorrow worn faces, and soothe them into sleep: oh, the awful truth of that! I cannot—could not, give up that world of my love: I do prosaically believe in it, as I do in the electric force. But then—Christ lives! lo, he is alive for evermore! alive, near me, by me as I write: his eyes may have read this before yours do. When I laugh, he is my laugh: if I am disconsolate, he is my anodyne: and Shelley is with him, and Plato, and Dante hand in hand with Beatrice. They are Spirits: with identity of love and goodness: not themselves, but each his brother! each (logic) God. So that prayer is a true thing: Christ, have mercy upon us! Aye, and he tells us how he had mercy in his audacity of indiscrimination on an adulteress. Oh, what matter it whether I pray to Christ or a dead dog? both are live spirits now.

England and, I think, the world, wants Christ more than other spirits, tho' his brothers. You will let me just talk a little about him to a few souls before I go to him and Shelley, and receive their kiss?

Gaiters: convocation: the Book: the *Church Times*: the Bishop of Manchester: and the House of Lords.

What of these? why, a soul that wants to be exulted above the stars cares nothing for them: you must see how absolutely unimportant these things are to affect my position in the Church of Christ.

Browning thinks 'that Shelley would in time have come to accept the religion of Christ.' Yes! if he ever rejected it: which is a point. Tell me what you mean to do when you meet with Rachel in Rama: with

Songs of the Shirt,[1] with cries of the children: with grief and pain in every form? will you say, 'I love you: all is love: I can't give you reasons for godliness, but sanitation is the next best thing: be cultivated: 'beauty is truth, truth, beauty'. Is that your gospel to the lost of London?

I will tell them of a land of Infinite Pity, where Sin is a virtue, where Love means peace with brothers: where all will, must come, purified: I will not take upon myself the 'science of theometry';[2] nor give geography's aid to my land: if they ask me, where is it? I will say, in your hearts now: after Death, hearts are love and spirits whole.

Why do we live, unless to live again? Do we sin against nature, by not developing? We must develop: did the last gorilla think to himself: 'I am about to become man: I know all about it'?

So we know not; but we, being higher, can have intuitive certainty of development. Your 'Higher Pantheism' is on my side: 'Saul' is on my side: Darwin is with me. And you — ?

Spirits, numberless, aureoled with love, garmented with compassion, scientifically exact! spirits everywhere: the dead 'a-ticking like a clock':[3] And you an Athanasius contra that world?

Death and Love: why do you think that 'poets sing you fancies' about these two? surely there is a 'reason in nature'. Love is perfected in death: not by the cast-

1 Thomas Hood, 'The Song of the Shirt' (1843), a poem about the trials of seamstresses.
2 D. G. Rossetti, 'Spheral Change' (1881).
3 Elizabeth Barrett Browning, *Aurora Leigh* (1856), 'They've heard the Dead a-ticking like a clock'.

ing of the flesh, tho' that is a higher state, because it is the next state scientifically: (while we are fleshly, flesh is good): but love is perfected by the transition to the land of otherwhere, the land of dreams and fancies, where poets live, while yet on earth.

Why do you persist in thinking of these things as mere fantasies, beautiful imaginings? I tell you, they are actualities. No revelation is here needed: all savage races believe by instinct of stern logic in 'animism': a savage dreams of a chair: that must be a real thing: ergo, chairs have souls, true chairs for the spirit land! most rigid logic throughout.

(See Tylor's *Prim: Cult:*[1]): Try to think of what I say as truth for a day: see if it has no effect upon you. But, whether you believe it or not, I will not let you sell your birthright for the accurate hell broth of Positivist cooking: you are spiritual, and cannot help it!

Ever yours,
Lionel

I must send you a passage in Peacock's *Memoirs of Shelley*, which I quite by chance lighted upon after finishing my rhapsodies. Very significant: and before unknown to me.

1813

'He had many schemes of life. Amongst them all, the most singular that ever crossed his mind was that of entering the Church. We were walking in the early summer thro' a village where there was a good vicarage and garden........ he stood admiring it. The extreme quietness of the lane, the pleasant pathway

---

1 Edward B. Tylor, *Primitive Culture* (1871).

thro' the church yard, and the brightness of the summer morning apparently concurred to produce the impression under which he suddenly said to me—"I feel strongly inclined to enter the Church". "What," I said, "to become a clergyman, with your ideas of the faith?" "Assent to the supernatural part of it," he said, "is merely technical. Of the moral doctrines of Christianity I am a more decided disciple than many of its more ostentatious professors. And consider for a moment how much good a clergyman may do. In his teaching as a scholar and a moralist: in his example as a gentleman and man of regular life: in the consolation of his personal intercourse and of his charity among the poor, to whom he may often prove a most beneficent friend when they have no other to comfort them. It is an admirable institution that admits the possibility of diffusing such men over the surface of the land. And am I to deprive myself of the advantages of this admirable institution, because there are certain technicalities to which I cannot give my adhesion, but which I need not bring prominently forward?" I told him that I thought he wld find more restraint in the office than would suit his aspirations. He walked on some time thoughtfully, then started another subject, and never returned to that of entering the Church.'

A little unShelleyan: but very true and helpful to me now. The mere thought of the priest Shelley! God's priest, who rejected marriage, was expelled from Oxford, was branded and spat upon! Saint Shelley!

To change subject, tell Frank I go to gymnasium every day of my own accord, and am really developing somewhat, tho' yet no Hercules!

Pardon me, if you know my extract.

May 26

Compare my hierarchy with Comte's! What do you think of a few souls, elect, precious, mere memories and records, which my spiritual spheres filled with all dead things, where Christ and liars and tortured animals are together glorified: all equal, in glory and majesty? if you call my vision moonshine, what ever can you call Comte's monarchy of mighty memories but mere corpse lights to shew 'there lies a noble life: all dead now'!

I take up the orthodox 'arguments against infidelity': and I ask you, how do you propose to deal with practical, even vulgar sorrows and cares? Will you tell of beauty? of an ideal perfection in each man's heart, floating about the world, capable of union into consummate ecstasy of love? ah, so attractive, is it not, to the starving poor! it pays their rents and is warm 'against winter come'.

You fools everywhere!

Pardon me, if I am rather bitter, but I can tolerate no shams: and I see clearly that anything short of spiritualism is a sham, by itself.

Appeal to your own nature as it prompts you to believe or not. Don't you feel instinctively that a 'belief in ghosts' is a natural superstition, even if nothing more? I never disbelieve nature.

And the Church, perverted, protesting, reactionary, the Church is still the main witness to the truth as it is in Christ the truth of mystical revelations and holy visions. 'Credo quia ineptum! credo quia impossibile.'¹—that is, you might well take that position, the Romanist one: I take that of the idealist, the spiritual Emersonian. Combine all philosophies in one: think of Christ, Buddha, Swedenborg, Kant, Fichte, Jacobi, Emerson et hoc genus omne:² is there one of them but believes in spiritualism in some form? Is the little French professor with his smattering of sciences, a doughty dabbler in divinity, a greater man than these our fathers, who gave us the well, and we drank and our cattle?³

Lionel

30

College
May 30, [1884]

Dear Charlie,

I was waiting to hear from you: who had not written for ages. I knew you would like Canon King:⁴ I do not know him except in the pulpit: my people have often met him at High Church gatherings and the like. He is a splendid man: so are they all who are really priest, not ministers.

Poor Swedenborgian! reforming his creed! Why;

---

1 Tertullian: I believe because it is absurd. I believe because it is impossible.
2 And that whole category.
3 John 4:12: 'Art thou greater than our father Jacob, which gave us the well, and drank thereof himself, and his children, and his cattle?'
4 Edward King (1829-1910), prominent Anglo-Catholic and founder of St Stephen's House, Oxford.

how does he want it reformed? it is perfect, except *Heaven and Hell*. Do come down here to listen to God speaking through Knox Little: the man's face is better than a Fra Angelico angel. He will be here on June 29. I read 'Bishop Blougram' over for the third time carefully within a week last night, to verify my position: I think it is sound, even in Gigadibs' eyes: and the 'Death in the Desert'—well, that is 'so comfortable'.[1]

It is unspeakably lovely now: birds, sun, orchises, wild roses, warm growing grass: and the spirits so close, so very close.

Do you believe in 'movements'? Is the East End agitation a new one?[2] if so, can not some thing be done to make it a true and holy influence at work, by spiritual advance of thought? in short, by my gospel? I am conceited enough to believe it possible.

I see no new element in this sympathy with poor humanity, if you deprive it of spirituality: but a gospel of toleration; a proclamation of no sin;—that, with the spirit land, the Hereafter, wld be the leaven: and, with God's help, the lump should swell to cover all England. Dreams! but that is the right aim. A pitched battle with the devil, the Protestants, and the Positivists: what would come of that? I am hopeful: and, at least something must be the result.

If you think of it, the time is quite at hand for a new direction. Only consider: Tractarianism: Pre-Raphaelitism: Science: all things, have culminated

1 Robert Browning, 'Bishop Blougram's Apology' (1855) (a dialogue between Blougram and Gigadibs) and 'A Death in the Desert' (1864).
2 Inspired by revelations of slum conditions in publications such as *The Bitter Outcry of Outcast London* (1883), see letter 9.

into fixed lights now, steadily shining, as stationary as the live lights of the Renaissance and Reformation. There must be a new light kindled for our generation: and I am Comtist enough to believe that it will be a comprehensive one: only, not scientifically so, but rather spiritually: so that art, poetry, science, social ethics, κ.τ.λ.[1] will be as beautiful scintillations from the bright star of loving spiritualism, glowing in the sphere of Infinity. Is it merely rhapsody? but no: it is surely possible, and possibilities are growing facts.

And for this, we must take the Kingdom of Heaven—I mean, the Church of England—by storm. We must fill the Church with atheist priests, if you like: with Arians, Unitarians, anythingarians: but we must fill it. And then—we shall see what then. Circumstances will guide us, and we circumstances. Why not be a priest yourself?

We don't want logic and philosophy: especially the latter. It won't work. Emerson men laugh at, forsooth, as 'no philosopher': had 'no system': No! Emerson had no system: had Jesus? Eschew altogether the miserable affectations of Schopenhauer, Hartmann, Comte: hate all systems of that nature: but love the great idealists, Kant, Schelling, Fichte, Emerson. These are not philosophers: they are inconsistent, just as Christ was. Why, it is all quite simple:

Love produces suffering:

Suffering produces love:

round and round, along the ages, that is the spiritual ascension to God. I love: then I must see and feel pain, to feel my love. That is all. Why do you live?

---

1 Ktl, a Greek abbreviation equivalent to etc.

to be and do: i.e., to satisfy your nature and soul. In art and literature: as in toil: but still, always satisfy your being. If you sing, there must be a hero to be sung by you: if you are heroic, you will find yourself welcomed to the artistic hearts of inspired brothers. Interdependence: there is the secret of it all.

I wish you could love the services of the Church: pardon me, but I even think it would be an expression of love in you if you did. These glorious festivals we are celebrating now: the Ascension of Manhood into the Godhead: the Feast of the Holy Ghost, i.e., the consequent reception into Manhood of the divine spirit: oh, the ineffable loveliness of these things! You may say, 'Look what the Church makes of them: dogmatic unintelligibility'. No! some Churchmen do: not the Church.

Do realize the 'beauty of holiness' in the Catholic sense: the beauty of ecstatic worship: you will find it one of the nearest approaches permitted to the ideal Beauty of Plato. Man is a gregarious animal. The simple old truth is so useful: we must have churches—no, that is not it: we must have the Church, where 'all men may dwell'.[1]

Communion with God means visible love to man. The Church militant takes up the need, and becomes our mother so lead us to one another, so, to God, home.

Holy! holy! holy! holy means healthy. Do you not see, now? And beyond the death of the world, perhaps

---

1 Swinburne, 'Dolores (Notre-Dame Des Sept Douleurs)' (1866), 'O garden where all men may dwell'.

we shall see God, and know what Dante calls, the highest intellectual delight—Till then, we will love.

Ever yours,
Lionel

Do send me the inaugural paper of the 'Chatterton Club'. Good name: you know his confession of faith?

31

College
May 31, [1884]

Dearest Charlie,

At eight this morning I began to read your paper, very slowly: at nine I went to Chapel, and joined in singing the Athanasian creed: and now, at 10.30, I have finished your paper.

'This is the catholic faith.' that rang in my ears as I read the last sheets: and, strange to say, I was left with the impression that you and Athanasius were at one: 'except a man believe, faithfully, he can not be saved.' You are both right, in different ways: but the pathos of it, and the pity! Saved: and how? at the bar of our own hearts we bring ourselves to judgment, and give sentence on ourselves; for only ourselves know our own work, whether it be of God.

Do thy duty: be true: be loving: be joyous: be thyself, and not another—that is the creed of the world.

I would not throw open your arms to all Oxford: I think a great danger lies in that; the danger of public publicity: be, as you are, open to all the world, shirk nothing: but don't let in the world: I have a conviction that such holy societies as the Chatterton must be entirely composed of individuals who know each other perfectly, as friends may: reality and sincerity come that way. Tell me, if you will, who compose the society—that is, what Winchester friends, if any.

Poor Chatterton may be happy now—I hope so.

Do you know the lovely act of love which Catholic Churchmen practice: taking the Sacrament 'with intention'? I am just about the celebrate Jesus' death for all of you, in the spirit: praying that my Eucharist will avail for you by a double gift of grace? Words? surely not so.

Write when you have time, if you will.

Do come here on the 29th of June, as I said: do you think Frank would understand, if I said I would rather have you alone this time? don't either of you misunderstand me! but you won't, of course.

I will return your presidential baptismal inauguration as soon as possible. Read Ward's 'Clothes of Religion' in the *Nat: Rev:* and Stephens' 'The Unknown and Unknowable' in the *Nineteenth*:[1] both well written and sound sense. My hatred of Comtism is almost a monomania.

Do you know personally Scott Holland?[2] I only know *Logic and Life*, his voice, and his strange, sometimes beautiful face. How do these men believe? it would do you good to find out: Radicals in social and

---

1 Articles by Wilfred Ward (1856-1916) in the *National Review* and James Stephen (1829-1894) in the *Nineteenth Century.*
2 Henry Scott Holland (1847-1918), Anglo-Catholic and Christian Socialist. Lecturer and proctor at Christ Church, Oxford. Became canon of St. Paul's in 1884.

political questions: enthusiasts for science: holy and humble of heart: and stout Churchmen, who swallow creeds and gaiters with equal zest and believe in their efficacy. 'Is there a reason in nature?' I always pity poor Cardinal Wiseman, when I think of these men: he was one of them, born out of due time: and now he is quite happy at Rome. I never cared for Pusey and Wilberforce or even Keble: but the newer school, K-Little, Holland, Haweis,[1] King, and thousands more, are wonderfully attractive to me.

There is such an exhilaration in the growing physical strength! I go to gymnasium for an hour a day, and can now contemplate my blistered, hardening hands with less aesthetic disgust and more satisfaction.

I suppose Cruickshank is not one of you?[2] he always perplexed me here, when as a junior I studied him afar off.

I shall have but little time for about a fortnight, owing to 'Medals', i.e. prize compositions of kinds which take up time. I am enjoying myself with writing a poetical allegory by way of an 'English Essay on the Results of the Insular Position of Great Britain'.[3] The weather is too beautiful for practical thought.

Again thanking you for your paper,
Ever yrs,
Lionel Johnson

---

1 Hugh Reginald Haweis (1838-1901), fashionable East End preacher who insisted on compatibility of Spiritualism and Christianity.
2 See letter 21, fn.1.
3 Johnson's entry did not win (see letter 38), but he was successful in 1885.

32

College
June 6, [1884]

Dearest Charlie,

I am so glad: I shall not forget next Sunday, in the early morning. Oh, how wonderful a leveller is love! Neither bond nor free in Christ, who is Love: and God is Love: and Christ is a spirit now. Work that out to the end; you will find yourself so happy at the goal of life.

Do you know the volume of Shelley's *Letters* edited and prefaced by Browning, but withdrawn on discovery of their non-genuineness? there you will find Browning's opinion as to Shelley's Christianity. Yes: Aprile equals Shelley:[1] but only as the 'Suntreader' of 'Pauline' equals Shelley: both adumbrations of the Sun god of Love and Music.

I yesterday saw Matthew Arnold, whom I had seen but once before: a strange face, with too little tenderness to be quite loveable: not like Browning's expression when he is moved by anything, as music or his dead wife's poems. I am very dejected at your hopeless inability to come here: could you not possibly spare one day? but you can't, so I won't be importunate.

Scott-Holland's face shews how completely love can beautify things not of their own selves beautiful: his grotesque, Japanese features are simply lovely. I will really return your paper tomorrow: but I have been pondering on it long.

1 Aprile is an Italian poet in Browning's *Paracelsus*.

I had a dream last night: I was a priest of Rome, alone upon the Altar; and the chancel roof seemed to burst apart, and a chain of flowers swung down to me out of the blue, and as I tried to climb, I woke. Expound.

I have little time now: having to write verses for 'English Verse' on—Gordon![1]

Yours ever
Lionel

33

College
[June 1884][2]

Dearest Charlie,

With little better to do I write to you, hardly knowing why. I have felt so happily amused since Sunday, when the Second Master preached an excellent sermon, unconscious theosophy throughout: a masterpiece of priestly common sense and spiritualism: a delightful incident.

Why do people talk interminably about cricket? a topic so soon exhaustible and very dull: why will they bore their brothers so? at a school one can't avoid it much. What horrible profanity this thought reading

---

1 Major-General Gordon (1833-85), British Army officer who made his name in putting down the Taiping Rebellion in China in the 1860s and for his refusal to convert to Islam in early 1884, followed by the siege of Khartoum and his own death.

2 This letter was incorrectly dated May 1884 by Russell and sequenced before letter 27. George Richardson preached in Chapel on 8 June. See also fn.4.

is: or, rather, Stuart Cumberland's rejection of his own powers: it is quite dreadful altogether. I don't know what it tends to.[1]

Positivism ought to be rather down in the market just now: O Lucifer, Son of the Twilight![2] People are beginning to see that moonshine won't sustain life at any price: neither M. Arnold's Culture, nor Fred. Harrison's Humanity go down much: whereas Catholic Socialism and Spiritualism, being more tangible in their ethereality, are the hope of millions. Creeds and articles and dogmas are necessary: they need not be absurd intrinsically. I believe, on Mrs. Richardson's authority, that Frank is coming down for Eton Match:[3] if so, wld you tell him that I shall not be able to see much of him, as some of my people will be here, whom I couldn't well desert or introduce, alas!

What do people at Oxford think of Emerson, who seems by the critical faculty rather set in the ascendant? it is a sign indeed: but I can't forgive him for leaving his priestly orders, for the lecture desk.

I trust the Chatterton diploma work reached you. Do you know Ll: Davies' book on the Ephesians, &c?[4]

---

1 Stuart Cumberland (1857-1922) never professed to thought-reading, but claimed that a person might give away a thought by muscle reaction. Johnson refers to a demonstration given in the *Pall Mall Gazette* offices on 23 May 1884, in which Cumberland declared thought-reading without physical contact 'quite impossible'.
2 Isaiah 14:12: 'How art though fallen from heaven, O Lucifer, son of the morning! how art thou cut down to the ground, which didst weaken the nations!'
3 The annual cricket match between Winchester and Eton played 27 and 28 June this year.
4 John Llewelyn Davies, *The Epistles of St. Paul to The Ephesians,*

a splendid specimen of orthodox health.

I have been reading the Bp: of Ex:'s Bampton Lectures from newspaper reports:[1] they are very noble.

Ever yours
Lionel

34

College
June 22, [1884]

Dearest Charlie,

Thank you for the sight of your envied calligraphy after long silence. I have been unable to favour you with any specimens of hieratic hieroglyphs, through the claims of 'English Verse'. I think I have won a little insight into the boundless mystery of blank verse: the language and organ-tone of God and Shelley and Milton and Browning.

Of course you have seen poor Toynbee's book: and have digested his ideas on the relations of Church and State.[2] Cannot I be a priest of that Church and serve that Church? though, as you will have seen, he lays more stress on intellect and precision of logical formula than I should be disposed to do. But mysticism is now very popular with social reformers.

The Colossians, and Philemon (1866).
1 Frederick Temple (1821-1902), Bishop of Exeter, delivered 8 Bampton Lectures throughout 1884 at St. Mary's, Oxford, on the subject of the relationship between science and religion.
2 Arnold Toynbee (1852-83), historian and social reformer, wrote on 'The Ideal Relation of Church and State'. Published posthumously in *Lectures on the Industrial Revolution in England* (1884).

I, too, am going to leave an old home: and exchange the forests of Windsor for the wilds of Wales: otherwise, Flintshire: where, in an ancient and dilapidated mansion I purpose to study ghosts, who are 'authentic'.

I assent as to cricket: but it is an annoyance of intense pungency.

If you are really so wicked as to wed music to worthless words, might I say that my first thoughts are the best: and the omission of 'the while' improves sense and sound? I know Putnam's book: a very useful one for its purpose, as a contrary blast to Ingersoll and Bradlaugh; but a painful one otherwise.[1] Toynbee accepts both postulates: I do, in a sense.

I envy you your seclusion; though I am very self-contented just now, quantum mutatus![2] O Lucifer, Son of the Morning! and you abandon even in song the 'woes that no tears may stay'? but I am so glad, if it sent me your lines, which I return after copying.

I once had Toynbee pointed out to me in Oxford Street: and I know his face so well: I shall recognize him in the spirit-land before God points him out. Do you know Heine? I am revelling in the infinitude of his genius, in translations: but the infinite grandeur of his mockery! his work makes a deeper impression on me than most men's, except Dante. Do you care for 'Pauline'? Whatever Browning may think of it, he has never beating [*sic*] it in exquisite cadence and natural charm of description: two not characteristic things in

---

1 Samuel P. Putnam (1838-96) and Robert G. Ingersoll (1833-99), figures of American freethought.
2 How changed!

my God at all times. Just come from Chapel: heard a clever man and earnest priest eloquently propounding the duty of hating sin and abhorring evil: 'love is out of place in proximity to sin'. I was internally boiling: how can they be so monstrous?

So they reject Women's Suffrage?[1] do you know, I am almost glad? politics are too small things to engross Sappho and Mrs. Browning and Miss Rossetti and the Brontës.

June is perfect here: quite golden with soft air and blossoming limes and blue beyond: and more talk of 'Eton Match'! O tempora!

Am waxing incoherent: so will cease annoying.

Yours ever
L Johnson

35

College
June 26, [1884]

Dearest Charlie,

I take a guilty pleasure in writing to you instead of reading Thucydides' Browningisms: I feel polemically inclined tonight. As to the priesthood—you weaken your cause by your array of names: I take them individually.

Shelley believed in Christianity: by which I mean the story of the gospels, as a literature of practical

---

[1] The previous week the Gladstone government declined to add a clause on women's suffrage to the Franchise Bill, then being debated in parliament.

didactism: his own words are my argument, as I gave them you.

Emerson was ordained, wore surplices, preached: and, alas, turned his coat or rather, his surplice for his coat: but he upheld consistently the theory of priesthood: vide *Essays*, passim.

Toynbee says, 'I wish more young men would take orders: at present there is so much unwillingness.' As to the rest, their work is extraneous.

I protest now and always against your anti-Churchism: Baudelaire—no bishop's man—says, 'Christian sentiment and work are useless without a visible Church: brotherly cooperation is effete without an hierarchical organization.' What of that, most unpractical of iconoclasts?

The good Bishop of Rochester has turned a man out of the Church for denying the literal doctrine of the Resurrection, whilst confessing its mystical worth.[1] Now, I do not deny the literal fact: Christ rose the third day, to assure his disciples: for he was a Mahatma, adept, brother: you see? and so, why should I scruple to declare [I] believe in the dogma, and preach its significance? Your ideas are so unpractical: I wish I shook you by saying that religion is a corporate thing as well as an individual yearning: but it is true. Demoralize the Church! you talk like the *Church Times* of 'Erastianism'.[2] The Church must be

1 Russell added a rare footnote to this comment in *Some Winchester Letters*: 'Dr Thorold, afterwards Bishop of Winchester. He had inhibited Rev. Charles Marson for preaching a sermon saying that it was not necessary to believe in a literal flesh and blood resurrection'. See also letter 38.
2 The subservience of the Church to the state.

a state department, to be effective: granted your firm outline and skeleton, it remains to fill it up with individual aims and energies.

Of course I don't define sin: I can't sound a bathos. But does that affect my position? the Church, viewed as an aggregate of dignitaries, talks a fair amount of wild ridiculosity: but,—and this you forget—the Church means you and I and all men: and no Bishop can alter that fact. A poor man without a Church? think what that means, if you can. An uncultured man, with spiritual feelings undefined in the heart of him, crying out for love and help: and you come to him, *one man*, by yourself, and let your 'Christian sentiment babble love': and he is so comforted, is he not? don't you feel that to enter a Church is all the world to him: whereas individual love and Frederic Harrison and the Hall of Science[1] are nothing? you must feel that, if you have heart or soul. It is so real, so real, so urgent: I will be a priest.

Once introduce a spirit of toleration and love and pity instead of shudders and cold shoulders and shriekings, and all is done: then, in Laud's words, 'If the Church cannot stand, God help her: I cannot'. People say, 'You want vague philanthropy, differing from an -ism in state aid and surplices and endowments: we want dogmatic truth and precision of formularies.' Yes, people say that: people who give alms without a thought as to the bearing of the Athan: Creed on it: who love their brothers without the 39 Articles. Get these good people to be consistent, to test themselves by the rule of conduct: then the Church will be a home, not a hotel.

1 Secular lecture hall on Old Street, London.

I dislike Macaulay as a writer: respect him as a man. He maligns one of my heroes—Strafford[1]—and is a man of slippery antithesis: he never gets to the heart of anything above mediocrity.

I am behind the times, Radical tho' I be: I hate Women's Suffrage, because I hate politics as I do Protestantism.

I wish we were back in Greece: the perfect πόλις and ἐκκλήσια (forgive the unclassicism) then in one: neither 'demoralized'.[2]

Heine says, 'God, what is He? ah, He is merely the first person I meet in the street: even if he chance to be a creditor.' Oh, the infinite grandeur of Heine, the laughing Christ! do you notice how people say generally, 'artists and those people are very irregular': and pardon it at once: but you or I must be so strait laced before the world! how full of meaning that is, if you catch my thought.

No more time,
Ever yours (and God's)
L Johnson

Pardon writing: attribute it to dread of the next two days and anticipation of the third: Eton Match and Knox-Little!

Promise you will be present at my ordination: and promise to hear my first sermon and take God's body and blood from me. Because it will assure me of many things.

---

1 Thomas Wentworth, 1st Earl of Strafford (1593-1641), Royalist supporter and authoritarian Lord Deputy of Ireland.
2 Polis and ecclēsia, or state and church.

36

College
July 7, [1884]

Dearest Charlie,

Your lovely lines will live in my heart as assuredly as your letter will die there: you don't shake my position at all: calling a surplice a bib won't do it.

Your sole flash and glimmer of reason—pardon me!—appears when you talk of prayer. You are wrong: wrong utterly and miserably: but with a sensible, somewhat earthy wrongness. Do you forget a certain altar in Athens of the Agnostics?[1] Surely, if a man recognizes an 'Infinite and Eternal Energy': if a man accepts inscrutable darkness as the veil of the Unknown: yet his recognition and acceptation imply prayers for rain and the Queen. A paradox? Oh no! a bathos perhaps, somewhat pathetic.

Are you so content with the things that are, that you will try to set them right, and yet will refuse to send your soul on the wings of Love into the thin air of the void, in search of the Unknown? prayer is merely life: merely the outward expression of vital spirituality: O ye of little faith! If you could but know how intensely I long for the new birth of the Church: how I yearn after my dear vision of a high State Church, the grandest embodied House of Commons, the temple of Liberty, the Liberty of the children of God: how I

---

1 In Acts 17:23, Paul remembers passing in Athens an altar 'To the Unknown God', or Agnōstos Theos.

see the land, our loved English land, blossoming with fair shrines, thrilled with divine music and all beauty! you would be on my side, if only you knew my heart! Ah, how wretched you are, you spoilers of the people: but I stand in the front of time with eighteen centuries beside me. Leave the Church! I would as soon leave off to read Shakespeare and Shelley! what do you give us instead? see now! the Churches emptied of us priests: the Bibles torn away: let the King of Glory come in, the new Evangel of Shapeless Love and faithless Doubt! I can but repeat—the Church cannot be left alone: outside of it we can only seem hollow prophets of vain things. And you dare to speak of the poor man's love of Christ's Church as you would of his filthy slum: as a thing 'education' will rid him of! yes, and it will give him the *Principles of Psychology*[1] to read and teach his children: yes, and he will say, 'I will not beat my wife because the laws of sociology disallow it'. What! will you dare to lay a hand upon a human soul?

Of course it is all so hard: and you accuse me of taking the 'easiest way'! Ah, is it easy to preach Love and escape censure? to speak of Spirits, and avoid abuse? is it then so easy to conquer Bishops of Rochester by love and faith? to stand before an infidel world in a priestly garb and before a narrow Church in the guise of a man? Oh, if this be easy, truly I have chosen the easy way. But I tell you that at times of dejection I well nigh shrink from the burden of it: I well nigh am content to preach the easy doctrines of formless chaos lit with moonshine and lucifer-matches! But, thank Christ, I am ready: I will be a priest.

---

1 Herbert Spencer, *The Principles of Psychology* (1855).

I meant, is it not significant, that whilst common folk are expected to be 'moral', much is pardoned to 'men of genius'? as if 'genius' was free from law by its own right? I mean, does not the world seem content to own the inferiority of morality to art whilst praising it where art is not? fallacious, on both sides: but very full of thought. Think of Sappho, Catullus, Marlowe, Heine, Villon: and then of Smith and Jones.

Judge of what an effect your letter has on me, when I say that it read like Voltaire or Bradlaugh: 'see if these things are so!' how can you? and is it worth while at all? do 'Christian evidences' feed orthodox souls? do unbelievers find their prop in 'A Refutation of Deism'?[1] no! both live by the inner spirit. Suppose that Church gone: what remains? think what she is to the land: not only a clog, but also a guide: and if we might control the Church at all by taking the Consecration of her hands, what could we not try to effect!

In what way do I perjure myself? what assent do I give to things I disbelieve? if you think of the priests of England in the past, you will find place for me: by the side of Chaucer's vicar and Chillingworth and Hooker: oh, my conceit through Christ that strengtheneth me!

Among the voices of this world, the cries of soul-grinders on the whetstone of hard logic: the shrieks and sobs of shocked Pharisaism: the shouts of blatant Nothingarians: the sweet inanities of embryonic fancies: among the wails of mourners yearning into space and time after the light of dead eyes: ah, will you not let me break God's silence with one more

---
1 A dialogue by Shelley (1814).

word: peace? let me stand upon the altar steps in fair raiment and say one word to be borne away through glowing windows into the beautiful world: one word of love and peace and hope: and if you wish, I will keep to myself the struggles I cannot kill: struggles against hard stones and flowerless thorns of your grafting and throwing.

Faith! up to the land of stars and dead faces and throbbing hearts! faith! up to the embodied love of God, known but in Death! up to God.

Yours ever,
L Johnson

37

College
July 10, [1884]

Dearest Frank,
   At last.[1]
   I can't write at length just at once: work is so ex-

---

[1] Johnson's father rescinded his ban on his son's correspondence with Russell in the following letter dated 19 July 1884:
'I must write to thank you for your letter and to say how very glad I am to be able to rescind the veto I felt obliged to put upon Lionel's correspondence with you.
You are aware why I thought it best for Lionel that he should discontinue such very close intimacy, having been warned that it might tend to the unsettling of his mind on religious matters; I think, however, I may now depend upon you both and trust I may never have reason to regret the confidence I place in you. I sincerely hope that the renewal of your intercourse may lead to the happiness of you both, now and hereafter'.

acting. Thanks for Browning, to me unknown: true, largely: just a little too systematizing.

I return my father's letter: a reasonable one and straightforward.

What of the Bishops? the tide of many things is turning.

Must go off to Glee Club, and realize Immortality.[1]

Ever yrs

L. Johnson

P.T.O.

One thing in yr: letter I will answer: yr: remarks as to my expressions of failure, remorse, κ.τ.λ. Ah, they are and were merely incidents in soul-life: am I a God, to live for ever in changeless complacency? no, only a man: so, whilst I reject all right and wrong in themselves, surely I may still rule my life as I might carry out a fancy. And see—I live in the age of the 'Weltschmerz'.[2] I do no wrong: am I therefore ever happy? true, my sorrows never come from consciousness of wrong: but from the vague shadow of unrest thrown over life by passing things: 'a death, a chorus-ending.'[3]

See! Christ conceived as very personal God is still the Man of Sorrows: not an Epicurean Lotus-God. And Christ was—to the world's vulgar mind and tongue—sinless.

1 A secular rather than religious choral club.
2 Melancholy or world-weariness.
3 Quoted from memory from Robert Browning's 'Bishop Blougram's Apology', 'some one's death / A chorus-ending from Euripides'.

38
To Sayle

College
July 16, [1884]

Much writing hath made thee mad, dearest! Can you imagine me angry with you or anything? I merely smile when you sweep me away from the altar down the tide of vacuous and beautiful moonshine—Angry? oh, how foolish! Come, to Domum,[1] and don't think about disobeying me: beside, thou inconsistent one, how unchristian not to meet an angry brother! risum teneas, amice?[2]

I can't possibly come to see you elsehow: my time is literally filled up—so you must come, you see?

Have you been expecting an answer? well, I have written one, but won't send it: I will instead invite your attention to the fact that Rochester has recalled Marson without recantation.[3]

I won't be able to see much of you, I'm afraid: the end of the half is so busy.

I am now so elated: I have failed to get the English Verse, because 'tho' my poetical powers are far superior to the prize man's, and my metrical skill remarkable: I was not practical: I was too up in the air.'[4] there!

---
1 Breaking-up ceremony at the end of the school term.
2 Can you help laughing, friend?
3 See letter 35, fn.1.
4 See letter 31, fn.5. The English Verse prize went to Joseph, who also beat Johnson to the Moore-Stevens Divinity Prize (letter 14,

isn't that enough to intoxicate! rejected, on account of ethereal lightness and unvulgar impalpability! I am so conceited.

I can give you a ticket for Concert here: as a member of 'Glee Club' I have some at my disposal.

I won't let you off—so don't try.

Was my letter very scarifying? that is a compliment to me.

I am really sorry if I did hurt you at all: or rather hurt your prejudices, if I may say so.

Yrs ever,
Lionel

39

College
July 20, [1884]

Dearest Frank,

I really found no time last week to write to you: but I despatched a missive to Charlie requesting his presence for Domum. I am writing solely on practical matters.

1. Are you coming down for certain? if so, as I imagine we shld: travel together, what train? I want to know for Dick's sake: he always wants early information on these points.

2. How do I get to Willesden from you? I hate looking at Bradshaw, because they get it up so vilely.

Pardon my enquiries, but answer them as soon as you can.

---

fn.3).

'Yes, it's a very beautiful poem, a very good poem, but I don't see much Gordon in it.' Fearon's verdict: true as to the latter part: Joseph got the medal.[1] I really am quite glad: it is an incentive to action to be told one is too unearthly to succeed. I mean to work at poetry in Wales.

I do wish this half were well over: I do so loathe Domum day: and exams are wearing.

The Daker's sermon was splendid: 'platitudes of pious imbecility' &c; you would not have liked it: it was in my direction; entreating young men not to leave Christ through disgust at Christians: if our Xty is different from the world's, it does not follow that it is beautiful and false: rather beautiful and Christ's truth, i.e. his Church's truth.

What cowards—pardon me—you men are, who are frightened by gaiters and shovel hats: consider, Christ (I am not irreverent) wld wear them, if he were on earth.

I don't remember your correct address at Richmond: so send this to Dover Str:[2] —

Yrs ever,
Lionel

---

1 Johnson refers to his entry for the school's English Verse prize (see letter 38) and the fact that the Queen's Gold Medal for Latin Verse also went to Joseph. The Silver Medal for English Essay (see letter 31 fn. 5) went to Herbert Albert Laurens Fisher (1865-1940), who later authored many historical texts.
2 Pembroke Lodge in Richmond Park was the home of Russell's paternal grandmother, Lady John Russell; his maternal grandmother's London home was 40 Dover Street.

40
To Sayle

[July 20, 1884]

In haste, during the press of exams: dearest, thank you for coming: you will find the place in a frightful state of abominable confusion and me nearly dead with worry of kinds.

Tell me by what train on what day you will be here—if possible I will meet you.

Addio,
Lionel

You will hear fairly good music—nothing 'sacred' tho' nothing unworthy of the name of music.

What a dreadful thing a scholar is! and how I loathe scholarship and exams. I mean to work at poetry in Wales.

41

College
July 22, [1884]

Dear Frank,
Just back from Glee Club, too late for post. Would 7.23 suit you? I do feel so brain-wearied here amongst scholastic anxieties: but I don't care really.

Praise God for Rochester restored to health.

I will meet you on Monday in Cathedral.

Do you care for Domum Day? I do in spirit, but never in practice: those wearisome speeches and hateful dinner and lingering in-demand in chambers till 2 a.m.—I hate it all: shall shirk dinner and speeches, unless you care to go. Read the last *Sat: Rev*: on 'Esoteric Bosh': and tell me if it is true in any particular.

Can write no more.

Yrs,
Lionel.

42

Rhual[1]
August 8, [1884]

Dear Frank,

Having but just returned from exploring Chester, I have only now got possession of Walt Whitman, for whom take as much thanks as you will: he was almost thrown at me with a remark in Welsh by the Welsh postmaster as I walked through Mold, where a primitive cattle fair was rampant; so, the place being unconventional, I opened him on the spot, and read through the streets to the accompaniment of bellowing beasts and Welsh execrations: an appropriate scene. I am very idle here: write a ferocious tragedy in the woods, and make the acquaintance of the natives who can speak English. Shelley was beautifully wrong when he refused to extend his charity to anything coarse and earthily unrefined: they had his pity and abhorrence,

---
1 A house near Mold in Flintshire, Wales, which the Johnson's rented from relatives.

not his love. To me, Whitman is the nobler priest, who can declare to the world such confessions as verse 24 of 'Song of Myself', verse 48, 'Native Moments', 'You Felons', &c. Shelley would have the world ruled by the perfect freedom of love, but not this world, not the world of rude sensuality and earthiness, but a world among the stars where the air is too rare for anything but spirit: Whitman takes this world and shews that nothing is common or unclean: not even uncleanliness. I hardly think Shelley's the higher ideal because it is the easier: do you know Faust? Mephisto: can ridicule the Shelleyan 'yearning into the infinite' but when Faust begins to drain waste lands and accept the world, he is beaten. When you are happiest, you feel most inclined to treat things with favour: you find that your joy is dependent on the acceptation of the world as it is: ugliness' self becomes less intolerable: so the universal of happiness would be the absolute equality of act and word by the pervading uniter, Love. Who are you to say, 'This disgusts me, is therefore wrong'? Don't be vague: Love, if loving, has no limit save itself. Is this mere laissez-faire, mere idleness, mere self-satisfaction? God knows, it means hard struggling.

Poor Mark Pattison must be happy now with Scaliger and Grotius: I had rather be in hell with Shakespeare.[1]

Are you working? and do you love Lucretius otherwise than in Tennyson?

---

[1] Mark Pattison (1813-1884), rector of Lincoln College, Oxford, died on 20 July. He was working on a biography of Scaliger when he died.

I came across some Comtists lately who claimed Walt Whitman for their priest and heirarch: worse than the orthodox who set up pretentions to the exclusive possession of Jesus.

Is Gordon still too strong for you, or too weak to yield a meaning? either way, I don't care: and that is the right spirit in which to view one's attempts at poetry; and how delightfully conceited it makes one.

Do you know Wilkie Collins' *Heart and Science*, a powerful novel directed against Vivisection and Professor Ferrier in especial? tell Charlie to read and inwardly understand. I love doing nothing but exist: one can't annoy oneself.

Shelley's death does more to make one doubt the existence of a personal God than most things: no one but a Jewish Jehovah could have allowed it: and think what masses of vulgarity in Church and State and Society and Literature he would have saved us if he had continued writing for twenty years more: how absolutely barren English affairs were from 1822 to 1850: bar Browning, Reform Bill and Tractarianism and Tennyson, what good thing was there in all England? but perhaps it is 'all for the best'; though I don't see how.

Is Jowett at all on the road to death or retirement? Oxford has had enough of shams for a time and I want some change from 'the Balliol School'.

Have no more inclination to bother you.

Ever yrs,
L.

43

Rhual
Aug 14, [1884]

Dearest Charlie,

I would have written before this, but have been too absolutely dreaming and indolent even for that: For your letter I thank you.

I am trying to write in front of an exquisite miniature of William of Wykeham:[1] it prompts me to aspire to Canterbury: I should like to wear a mitre and dyed garments from Bozrah[2] or Rome. Frank has just treated me to some vulgar inanities about being an Independent minister: oblivious of things temporal and ignoring things eternal: if he, following a rational impulse, wants to adopt sacerdotalism, let him do it beautifully at least. Will you ever understand what I really, seriously mean when I talk of the Church? I want, pre-eminently, a public setting forth of beautiful acts and emotions: and beauty means the fusion of spirit and sense. Next, I want the mass of my brothers to be able to feel that they are one in Christ or Shelley or Buddha or Hugo: one, as men living under equal, natural laws, and subject to like passions and aspirations and sufferings: i.e., I want Corporate Love. Required, then, the means of outwardly showing in the most spiritually and sensuously beautiful forms the incarnate reality of Corporate Love. Words, mere

---

1 Founder of Winchester College and New College, Oxford.
2 Isaiah 63:1, 'Who is this that cometh from Edom, with dyed garments from Bozrah? this that is glorious in his apparel, travelling in the greatness of his strength?'

words, till I can find a means; hence, I look around me: and I see an ancient Church professing Christ as her head, with certain practical government and articled faith: with Shelley for polestar and Whitman for pilot I accept Bishops' tithes (a hard stumbling block), 39 articles, even Lord Penzance: believing in none of these things, caring for none, if you throw them at me as facts: but thankfully taking home as painful yearnings after light these well nigh vulgarities, and refusing to set the world's trivialities as rocks of offence in my own way. And you, professing belief in Shelley, accuse me of 'perjuring my conscience': I make bold to alter the expression into 'sacrificing my prejudice'. Because I swear, I must be perjured: because I submit, I must be fettered; because I do not reject, I must welcome: is this your logic, ye of absolutely no faith?

Plainly, I, being a human brother of millions, humbly long to leave the world none the worse for my presence, if not better: and I am not so proud as to be an 'Independent Minister' when I might be an altar-priest pleading with—God, is it, or Fate or Nothingness?—for the woes of helpless men and women and little children.

Do you ever find a true Churchman placing his Bishop's gaiters before his blessing, his shovel hat before his laying on of hands? well, perhaps you may: at least, hat and gaiters are not other than strong fastnesses against the strong tide of Nothingness. Oh, you pseudo-humanitarians who minister to your brother independently of aught but self: who cling to Little Bethel but abhor Cathedrals because the Chapter House and Canon's precincts are too close: you who strain at the gnat of harmless formularies and gulp down open mouthed the vulgar moonshine (excuse confusion of metaphor) of dissent: will you ever be seeking after a sign and eschewing the example of Jonah, who had scruples, doubtless conscientious, against preaching in Nineveh, because it was a dangerous stronghold of false and foolish and venomous idolatry: yet who speedily went and made that same city repent—a city, oh the pathos, which held so many little ones, who 'knew not the right and the left', and 'also very much cattle'?[1] poor Nineveh, with its fat oxen in prebendal stalls and little children who knew not the Bishop of Manchester from Mr Green: poor Nineveh, going to the bad whilst you are independently tossing on waves of your own arousing: poor wicked Nineveh!

Truth as an absolute known quantity or quality is not to be found: Mme: Blavatsky[2] may have found it in miraculous teacups, but hardly so as to preach it in Westminster slums: unfortunate slums, given over to the tender mercies of Monsignor Capel and Henry Edward.[3] I cannot now—think, if you will, I am shirking difficulties—go into detail of doctrines, 'inhuman doctrines never taught by John'[4] but to be found vaguely inside the bounds of a prayer book: I have done so abundantly to my own satisfaction. I have one monotone to which I will intone my life: 'I will be a priest': not, you may think, the music of the

---

1 Jonah 4:11.
2 See letter 3, fn.1.
3 Thomas John Capel (1836-1911), a Catholic priest who went through a highly publicized scandal concerning his personal morality. Henry Edward is Cardinal Manning (1808-92).
4 Elizabeth Barrett Browning, *Aurora Leigh*, book 1.

spheres: but at least, not out of tune. I (this epistle is egoism itself) I hope to be ordained Deacon in the year 1888 or 89: to remain, if possible, in a fellowship or the like; at Oxford for a few years: and then to have a 'cure of souls': I long for an unsophisticated parish by the dear sea: in Cornwall or Norfolk or Devon: or anywhere. To live in seclusion, writing for my bread, and living as one of the common herd: infusing beauty and the simplicity of love, the ideal of Christ or and Shelley, into minds fresh from God and the great sea. And after that, twenty years of such work, I should wish to come into more constant contact with masses of hereditary misery and want: to wear out the rest of my life in 'our great towns'. What an ambition! sincerely, what an almost inconceivable aim: and oh to realise it. You may come and hiss at the parson and the state Church and the fat livings: I thought Christ observed the Jewish law: you, the independent Christs, may trample the beautiful Church because bygone νεωκόροι[1] have omitted to cleanse it from the mud flung at the carven wood of the sanctuary: nay, from the foolish accretions some of themselves accumulated in Georgian days, when ladies wore patches and the Church wigs. William of Wykeham is smiling at me now with his beautiful mouth and eyes from under the weight of the jewelled mitre: and I take the blessing of his three symbolic fingers. I don't remember his being an independent minister: but he did shelter incipient Lollardism.

What wild hysterics I have been writing, so far as you are concerned and Frank: of course you will both

---

[1] Neōkoroi, temple custodian.

be Church of England priests and show the Positivist Society that Auguste Comte was a well meaning fat Frenchman whom God, being a little giddy just about that time with what his world was about, forgot to make into an Archdeacon.

I may be mad: I'm not bigoted.

Ever yrs
Lionel

44
To Sayle

Rhual
Aug 20, [1884]

One thing, Charlie, thou lackest: sell all thine Eternities and give to the poor: and don't go away sorrowful. You steadily shut your eyes to the fact that you can't preach capital letters without illuminating them in purple and scarlet and gold: you can't preach without a pulpit. You need not draw my attention to the existence of Goethe and Emerson and Ruskin and the other gods: they may dispense with pulpit if they like, and be satisfied with the intelligent appreciation of the cultured classes: but I, who am no demigod with a new evangel, but merely a man talking to men, will take what vantage ground I can. For the truth is that if you once think of the meaning of the world and time and the stars, your Eternities and moralities look as small as my Church: and I, being as I say a man, am not above using practical methods. For observe: I do not know the word 'morality': or the word 'immorality' or the word 'sinner' or the word 'saint': my ideas are not exalted, perhaps, or noble, and I am terribly on the side of worldliness. When I write a Sonnet, do I reflect that there is something trivial and uninspired in sitting down to shape my thought into fourteen lines of sestet and octave? well, Whitman does: but, as I have told you, America is not England: and I would not be a priest there. You may be of Paul, you may prefer Apollos, but I am Christ's: and preach him as I best can.

Sensuality, or rather vulgar indifference to the spirit of the senses—how to treat that in connection with ritualistic appeal to the senses.

Well, I hardly know if I grasp your meaning: beauty, you say, is right as a manifestation of God and a means of appealing to the outer man: but what of it in re God? Well, 'Beauty is Truth, Truth Beauty, that is all ye know on earth, and all ye need to know.' Is Keats right? When I absorb the soul and love of a picture, I worship; when I bring another to it, I have done the priest's office; I dare not pry into a strange soul: for 'we mortal millions live alone'.[1] The world is very good and the melancholy of it and the pain: God is glorified in these. Love and Truth and Freedom—are these things high and holy? then they will be powerful in the world and make it like themselves. Many messages have men syllabled and laboriously evolved to men: I speak the words of Christ and 'take away the sins of the world': not by redemption, for Christ did not barter with a personality: but by saying, with Christ, 'I take away sin'. To me it seems so strange that

---

1 Matthew Arnold, 'To Marguerite' (1852).

you should think it possible to effect real change in the world but by the power of the priesthood: you are not priests till the Bishop of Rochester or Gloucester have ordained you: you may be priests by the eternal holiness of capital letters, by the consecration of your own ideals: but you are not priests to men. I am perfectly in earnest: this earth is full of facts, and my principles will not let me despise or ignore any thing: in Germany I should turn my soul into metaphysics: in France into Victor Hugo; in Italy into—well, itself: and in England, into sacerdotalism. It's the one, old argument: reach the people, get hold of the world as you can, don't be exclusive, or found religions: preach love and pity and indifference. How? in what way is to you most able to be powerful: by the power of beauty and love visible in ecclesiastical tailoring if you will, and priestly haberdashery. And is this a low standard, and so I fall so very far below Shelley in my ideal? for I do not say to the drunkard, 'drink if you will, I don't know why you drink: I won't presume to dictate: I love you' but 'brother, can I help you?'

You see, I can't spend my life in getting together a Church and founding a sect or party: I find my means ready at hand, and use them. I know what Mazzini taught: I know how Emerson is not apparently for me, and that Goethe would not applaud me: but my spirit justifies itself. At least, I can do no wrong, for I know not what wrong is. The Church is catholic: Christ made her able to rear the nations in her bosom. Men shall be told that they may be sensualists, liars, cowards, worldlings, even vestrymen, and yet men as high as Christ. My Church may reek with the fumes of wine and cigars and ring with the cries of gambling hells and brothels: 'Behold the Lamb of God, who takest away the sins of the world'. I work for and in the present, because I am a fatalist, otherwise, a believer in evolution. If you can make men who are immoral, trivial, careless, believe that the world is holy by their human presence, that love is the great leveller, I will leave you to preach Love to the few elect. I best know my own powers: and I know the Church is what I want. Can you see nothing but shams in my ideal, because it cares not a jot for Eternities, i.e., sees Eternities where you see miserable pretence?

I don't think the real life that has moved on the earth's surface since the days of the mastodon has at all varied in real character: always gay carelessness, high seriousness, and law moving through all and in all. 'Think of many things': of Greece, of Japan, of the Pampas, of Lapland, of London, of Castle Howard:[1] is not life mainly the same? the future developments of the world I neither know nor greatly care to know: at least I see my own age. Don't say that I choose the smooth path: to justify the ways of Bishops to man is appalling in its hopeless immensity of labour: to wear white robes before men is to provoke mud throwing. I am just a piece of life, as is a dog or a railway porter or the Mahdi: let me live my life as I will. To write 'poetry': to preach my own crochets: to love men and women and hate capital letters and H more than any: there is my life.

---

1 Castle Howard, York is the ancestral home of the Howard family. Russell's Aunt Rosalind was Countess of Carlisle, wife of the 9th Earl, George Howard. Russell and Sayle were staying with them at the time of this letter.

You may be 'free among the dead':[1] or free among the unborn: I prefer to be free among the living: chacun à son goût.[2]

Whitman would let me seek ordination at the hands of a bishop or else abjure his own principles: am I inconsistent? very well then, I am inconsistent. If you want to strip me of priestly clothing, show me that the world of ignorant peasantry, vulgar bourgeois, and ridiculous aristocrats will refuse my preaching: till then, don't try. Of course the clouds would object to my surplice: but I am not in the clouds. Pilate was wise who 'would not stay for an answer'.[3]

Ever yrs
L

45

Rhual
August [28, 1884]

Dearest Frank,

I know I should have written before this to you and Charlie: in fact I wrote to him long ago and forgot to post the letter: will do so now. You see, poetasters think themselves more of consequence than all else: and I am absorbed in my play, of which I have written 1200 lines, and I am deeply interested in trying my powers: I really think I have read worse. It is intensely

---

1 Psalm 88:5.
2 Literally, to each his own taste; English idiom, to each his own.
3 Francis Bacon's essay 'Of Truth' (1597) begins 'What is Truth? said jesting Pilate, and would not stay for an answer'.

wretched, and hopeless: and I call it 'Miserabilia'. And really nothing else now interests me at all, not even the Church.

Thanks for your past lucubrations: according to my lights very interesting and attractive, but don't think me heartless, if I say, foolish: not that they need be so to you: I merely read, mark, and am scientifically observant. Of course the world would be rather mean if it accepted my views: but I don't think that a misfortune.

It is more in creating that one sees the truth of my gospel of commonplace and laissez aller: when I catch an exact cadence for my line, or find a subtle alliteration, or succeed in presenting a character, I know that morality is non existent: artists in verse and stone and colour will tell you otherwise, sometimes: but not the Gods. And my Church work would be the same: the reading of antiquated, picturesque prayers: the preaching heresies to one's brothers: the whole system of Church order, would be merely acts of independent creation: true, not absolutely free acts: but free, so far as I am able to use freedom: which point I have settled to my satisfaction. Just think: a man's life is not his acts of profession: drills, sermons, deathbeds, stone-breaking, are not the life: but accidents of the life: the life is the sunsets we worship, the books we read, the faces we love: the acts the world sees us perform, *need* not be the life: if I am a priest, yet my life need not be clerical and bounded by a stockade of gaiters. I live, by divine law which made me: just as music exists not as sounds, but a star, so I exist as free will and sense and spirit, not as a person swathed in surplices or wearing strange hats: I do not give up my freedom, that is the point, I am not bound and perjured and a liar: nor need you be.

At my worst moments I see myself Archbishop and Poet Laureate: at my best, I don't see myself at all, but merely God and other men and the world and my dear art. Do you see?

Practically, by the way: if you examine all existing, congregating Churches: Wesleyans, Calvinists, &c, you will lose where spiritual freedom is so perfect as in the Church. My brain is whirling with my last Act, and I can't write now: I have condensed my usual diffuseness.

Evys
L

46

Rhual
September 2, [1884]

Dearest Charlie,

I want to know quite definitely the precise points which 'your superstition boggles at' the formularies of the Church: what actual phrases you could not use as a priest without internal repulsion? I don't know what I believe: I don't want to believe more than I feel: but then, I feel the beauty of anything, even of the αὐτό κάκον.[1] I intend to be inconsistent and tie you down to logic: what is it in yourself that says No to any religion? surely not absence of faith, unless you still cling

---

1 Auto kakon, evil in itself.

to miserable Mill: which I suspect you do in spite of yourself: there is in his dry, barren wastes of exact prose a terrible fascination. Once know for yourself—nothing can teach it you—that matter is non-existent, that idealists are right, that spiritualism is right, and I am unable to see what can keep you from turning priest or parson or God on your own account. You stop before such atoms in the sun beam, and pore over them with microscopes of logic and unreason till they swell to fill the whole sunlight—there's enough dreadful light in the world without artificial twilight.

Do you think that you are where you are and what you are, that you may 'live alone'? naturally, not so: then, if not alone, with your brothers altruistically: i.e., on their terms: and the terms of most English folk are 'Church and State': you believe, perhaps, as I do, in Love and Liberty, κ.τ.λ.: but we must say of Love and liberty 'They are all atoms in the void', and bow before Church and State: because we are loving and free when we do so, because we are humiliating ourselves, because we are walking through life in a series of inward shudders with smiles on our faces: because we are 'going up to Jerusalem to the feast', with Jesus, because we are 'shaving our heads in Cenchreae, for we have a vow' with Paul.[1] Disgusting, is it? well, disgusting = unpleasant to *our own* taste: I know my life must be greatly disgusting.

I want an answer.

I have written the last lines of my work: all I have done in the world of art is a horrible stack of poetastry

---

1 References to, rather than exact quote from, John 5:1 and Acts 18:18.

and a play of 1627 lines: but quite enough sins for seventeen. I have walked myself to death among the Welsh mountains, and am perfectly happy: I have also begun every sentence of this letter with 'I'. Are you resolved upon the London School Board? I think you would rather not bring Shelley there: haunt of ugliness and squalor and coal smoke, and the minimum of beauty.

Am getting illegible—
Ever yrs
L

If you ignore the Eng: Ch: as an existing force in England, you must fail: if you recognise it, where are you?

47
To Sayle

Rhual
September 9, [1884]

Has it ever struck you, dear brother, that you are very cruel to me? not that cruelty on your part can affect me at all, but from your point of view it must be harsh-looking. The ideal which I grasp at because it is so humble that it bears an air of puerile triviality, you elevate on the pure, white pedestal of your own aspiration, and label it as Liar, Jesuit, Insincere, Low, Mean, Deceitful: whereas in truth it is only Love. Why will you fling Articles, Gods, Trinities, Rituals in my path, and make me pay before each the toll of counterfeit assent? Must I '*lie*' to you (I don't know the word) and say, I believe the dogma, or to the world, saying 'Quicunque vult'?[1] Accepting your standard, your measure of moral definition, I will tell you that I am a liar and I am a hypocrite; that I take the smooth path to fat stalls, and court the fashionable appetite: that I am gloating over anticipated Passion Weeks and hungering after beautiful altars and perfect vestments: you intend cruelty, and I confess to you what you long to wring from me.

But you are wrong, wrong, and you are loved of me, and wrong in your thoughts. Myself know, I do not pose as a hero: as a man turned priest for others' good: but I know also that I am true. I tell you again, I see no means whereby the brotherhood of men in the whirling passion of life may be asserted but by joining men's hands: by bringing all men into one fold under one shepherd: and that shepherd, Jesus, Jesus, Jesus, and the brothers of Jesus. Ah, but I cannot do that: that means, you say, the empire of Love and Freedom over a world regenerate by Love and Freedom: that means drowning with Shelley. Does it, my brother? You may laugh: yet I think my part is not unworthy: you trample upon your dragons of superstition, mean audacity towards the unutterable one; and men will, many of them, and, (ah me!) the holiest of them, applaud you: I contend with articles of faith, with my lying conscience, with canonries, with poor material Christians: my voice comes 'choked with lawn sleeves', and caught away by incense and perfume: take your

---
[1] The opening words of the Athanasian Creed.

truth: you preach naked truth: I lie, that Love may abound. Too hard for you, is it? you will not swear falsely, you will not lie? but I, your brother, will do that, for Jesus's sake, and yours and all men's.

But perhaps this is Jesuitry again? I still hanker after a band of devotees: I still am emulous of 'the day's famous names': Scott-Holland, Knox-Little, Stanton, King, are my models? I lie so inveterately, you don't know what I mean? Charlie, perhaps that is not the least part of my burden.

Your last letter does not answer my objections: you say what I might say. I neither believe in the Trinity nor disbelieve: I neither believe in the Vice-regent of Christ, nor disbelieve: 'I cannot understand: I love'. 'Lo, here is God and there is God' true: everywhere: in conventicles and churches and open air: the whole mystery of life, and deep holiness of identity is too great for me: why should we solve it?

Ah, the pity of it: the men and women that walk the world at war, with want and woe beside them: all against all: and weeping Love wandering homeless.

But if I, bowing my head, say 'I know nothing: I feel love: and God is Love: He is somewhere, being Love: and everywhere, being Love: and perhaps all things are very good, for I dare not think I know' then, why may not I look around me, and discover Atheists, Mormons, Parsees, Buddhists, Catholics? and say 'of all these, which is best for my case, when I must work?' and, so saying, not choose the Church of England, hoping out of Her means to feed the poor? 'But you don't believe in Her doctrines: what She asserts, you deny: you are out of place if not worse', yes, all that is so: but then—can I stand up and say, 'I believe': or, 'I do not believe'? I do not know: I will make the best of it: were I to stand alone and preach aspirations of my own, the world wld be aloof and the stars would ask me 'Do you here know or believe?' Turn all ways: every way the same pathos of doubt and aversion: and we must do our best: the night cometh.

You cannot lie: you can love: but you cannot attain the sublimer heights among the night airs and grand stars, whither lying is your guide, hypocrisy your wings; you can love: you cannot lie. Lying is it? or merely Love in the dress of undisputing hope?

Still the old thought haunts me, clings about my mind; you don't know what I mean. Well, you are free: the world I must preach to must with a great sum purchase this freedom.

Are not my lying and my Jesuitry, the quintessence of Truth?

Yrs in hope,
L

48

Rhual
September 14, [1884]

Dearest Frank,

You must forgive me silence, if speech pleases better in this hollow prison vault of a world, where we fumble and grope in the dark to find the keys: death silences, and I have known death very near of late: my words to Charlie have been mere soliloquies I felt obliged to inflict.

I can hardly write anything now: my time in a house full of visitors is limited, tho' my mind is freer than usual, by intercourse with a dear friend and cousin.[1]

But I must write, if only to say that I am but too willing to congratulate you on the winning of a new member to your kinsfolk: 'how love is the only good i' the world!'[2] And now, having said all I can, I will merely utter the old cry I have so often uttered: will not you perjure (what does that mean?) our life, that many may become free indeed?

Love—love towards one, one alone, one in the world: what is this but love for all, if you think rightly? when a yearning stirs within the spirit to become one with a high, lonely star, to make two one, that unity may be the sole existence, then love of men and women is sprung to light out of dark hesitation: the single love is the myriad love isn't it so?

Can you find Truth? nay is there a Truth such as you seek? I think rather that the stress and play of life and emotion here is perfect in wisdom: 'good Will somehow be the goal of ill';[3] 'that's what all the blessed

---

[1] The cousin referred to throughout these letters is most likely Olivia Shakespear, née Tucker (1863-1938), later writer and lover of W. B. Yeats, to whom Johnson introduced her. Her daughter Dorothy married Ezra Pound.

[2] Robert Browing, 'The Flight of the Duchess' (1845). The engagement of Russell's paternal aunt, Lady Mary Agatha Russell (1853-1933), had just been announced. It was subsequently broken off when she became subject to insane delusions. She remained a lifelong spinster.

[3] Tennyson's *In Memoriam* quoted from memory, 'Oh yet we trust that somehow good / Will be the final goal of ill'.

Evil's for':[1] ugliness, pain: these are the serene notes struck from the organ-soul of God: nay, are God.

To create beautiful things where poor ugliness was: to seal kisses when society's Pariah-brand gloomed: is not this God? and you strive and battle after God, and do not win your desires. I tell you, be happy, for that is to know God: be sinful, for that is to feel God: be all things, for that is to be God. Don't think this is paradox, the antithesis of seventeen slight years: I tell you this is what you long to win: but you will not, nor would Jerusalem.

I can say nothing more until, perhaps, today week or fortnight: being fully occupied.

Evyrs
L

49
To Sayle[2]

[College
September 1884]

You will forgive the folly of words, where the heart only can speak? but last night there were stars, and a moon, and soft winds and airs, and love over all—and I want to thank you, however feebly. Angry? what is anger? I know love, and laughter, and pity, and interest—all these: but never anger.

---

1 Robert Browning, 'Bishop Blougram's Apology'.
2 The original of this letter is missing and is reproduced here in its 1919 published version.

50

College
September 21, [1884]

Dearest Charlie,

Coming out of Chapel after an ecstasy of radical sacerdotalism from Linklater, the priest of our Portsea Mission, I must say something. The sermon suggested a new idea and striking: civilization, art periods, monarchies, centres of thought, pass away into darkness, because they are disobedient to the science which requires bodies that would become live organisms to be quickened and then sustained from without by relation: i.e., the piteous efforts of humanity to be at one, to be able to love, to be tamed into unselfishness despite of themselves, must fail and have failed ceaselessly, because they do not infuse into their work a portion of that divine aether and love which ruled the evolution of each one of their units. Mankind, by nature (i.e., in Eden—vide Genesis) was harmonious: harmony was broken by discord, 'that harmony might be prized':[1] hence the social aims and propaganda of love, either red-dabbled in blood or thin with ghostly dearth, fade away, pass into the past: but the great unity of Christianity is the return to that state wherein life was one orchestra of sympathies, near to the feet of God: or, before Love met with ugliness. Am I clear? for the sermon was exceedingly arresting in its glimpses of early union between man and man and God.

---

1 Robert Browning's 'Abt Vogler' (1864) quoted from memory, 'Why rush the discords in, but that harmony should be prized?'

That I could tell you one fragment of the rhythmic life-march that I listen to in moments of silence and hushed beauty: when the world and the nations and the powers and the princedoms and the sinners pass through the gates of perfect temples hand in hand, chaunting their Trisagion of Faith, Hope, Charity: and the greatest of these is Charity: for God is Charity: Charity which makes the pure saint bow to the dust before the sinner, saying, 'Brother, love me, if thou canst, for thou art lovely'. Do you think my ears catch only the rustle of silk rochets, my eyes wish for the dazzle of scarlet hoods? if you so, you are yet in your sins.

Will you take the 'Metaphysics of Agnosticism' for your creed?[1] will you be good, because it is pleasant to be good? will you be compassed with a great cloud of witnesses? or will you rather love, and so win a God indeed; and, when you say 'God', you say, 'all that is, but not I'.

When the incarnation is helpful, I will preach it: when It alarms, I will pass It by: when It disgusts, I will deny It: wouldn't you, to help your brothers? Shall you think I am enamoured of paradox, being no true believer in anything? think that: have I a right to bid you think otherwise? you are you: I am I: we are not one, as men: but we are one, as broken sculptures from the infinite glories of the house of life not made with hands, now seeking to be rebuilt without cement by you and the world and the *Nineteenth Century Review*.

'But truth is truth: you can't say one thing and then another': dear brother, how strangely you limit

---

[1] Frederic Harrison published an article titled 'Agnostic Metaphysics' in *Nineteenth Century* (1884).

truth: do you remember Desdemona's deathbed lie? and do you shake your head over that truest of beautiful truths?

You had better give up persuading me: even though I see the men who might win a world to the arms of Love passing by on the other side: even then, I will try to do my best, while I live in the light: the night cometh, the night cometh.

Do you know the most awful utterance of man since man was? it is part of a Psalm of a Hebrew King: 'free among the dead'. Just try to think over that: the franchise of death, the wandering wills of shadow land, the freedom of helplessness: 'free—among the dead'. And you are free—among the dead: I (ah, the conceit) am bound that the living may be made free. Yes: take your dead citizenship: yes: join Socrates, be one with Voltaire: I am bound on the cross with Jesus, with Naaman in the House of Rimmon, with Bhuddha beneath the Tree; yes: take your freedom—among the dead, and leave us, for we are slaves.

Slaves: pass us by, waste no wine and oil: we are slaves, nay, I am a slave, for it seems I shall stand or bend down or lie down or writhe or die, alone, quite lonely: but what matters it, so my brothers live the enfranchisement of love, being made 'God-enfranchised souls'?[1] yes: free among the dead, free to flit shriekingly across the dusks and glooms of the twilight: free

1 Annie Chambers Ketchum's novel *Nelly Braken: A Tale of Forty Years* (1855): 'Circumstances arise sometimes though, which, despite what the preachers say, are not directed by Providence; and I feel almost angered when I see noble, God-enfranchised souls made slaves to them, from the mistaken opinions of the world, rather than the convictions of their own pure consciences'.

among the melting mists that flee away before the rising of the sun: I am a slave, who am bound in rusty fetters, whereby many are rejoiced.

Are you so very earnestly bent on cowardice, because you can't bolt a paradox which is only a truism?

Ever yrs (not mine)
Lionel

PART 3
BROTHERHOOD IS GOD

51

College
October 14, [1884]

Dearest Frank,

You must forgive me for not writing lately: I have been so entirely occupied: in a letter-writing controversy elsewhere, and editing the *Wykehamist*: every word of which I had to write, except the camping business. Will you write me an article on any subject you like sometime? I feel as if I should remain quiet mentally now, with my mind made up and my spirit satisfied: devoting myself to literature, wherein I intend to make presently a greater venture: I can't tell you in what way.

And now happiness does not seem treason to my suffering brothers: and life is friend to death, and sin to purity: all things are made new. In the interests of daily life, this faith proves itself: I can endure depression, vulgarity, Philistia, with calmness: absorption in metrical details and art systems does not appear merely dilettantism. And then, above all, there is the sense of sacrifice: sacrifice of personal freedom, personal irresponsibility: the Cross of Christ Jesus is a reality. I think you cannot live much without believing in the universality of holiness.

I have lately brought peace back to the mind of a very dear cousin: a girl on the verge of grown womanhood, and to me a revelation of my faith in the flesh: the labour of love is comfortable.

I can't write much: every thought is swallowed up in quiet content and inexpressible looking forward: I simply 'have nothing to say'. But write often, even if I can't always answer.

Charlie's 'In Memoriam' is very beautiful: in thought and expression: the latter, very quaintly beautiful.[1]

Tell me what you liked of my production? I ask as a self-critic: I am hard at work on poetry just now, with a hope of publication: conceit is coming fast upon me with, I think, growing strength: enthusiasm for what I hold as my art flourishes, now my eternal wants are asleep.

Tell Charlie I will write to him soon: but feel now constantly busied: you see, as a senior prefect, and Prefect of Chapel, and Ed: Wyk: and member of Mission Committee, κ.τ.λ., my time is well filled.

I have decided, selfishly, not to go up to Oxford next October, but the year after: I am right.

Excuse the inanity of my remarks: but I am actually unable to write.

---

1 The poem, for T. B. O. who died 10 Jul 1884, aged 22, was published in the October edition of *The Leaflet*.

I came back wonderfully strong, tho' my eyes are painful: I take care of myself.

Yours ever in love,
Lionel

My love to Charlie.

52

College
October 19, [1884]

Dearest Frank,

Thanks for letter.

I can perfectly imagine—indeed, almost feel from his letters—what you say of Charlie: but whilst I would wish it were not so, still, since it is there, surely it almost constitutes a charm? the apparent taint of worldliness that clings about him at times complicates his character delightfully, adding the element of entire surprise: I know this can't be a real comfort, yet from the Browning point of view, it is satisfactory enough.

You will come down at Christmas to Concert and bring him? We are singing Mendelssohn's divine 'Lauda Sion': some passages realise God; notably a grand outburst 'He sitteth between the Cherubim, be the people never so unquiet': each practice of it is to me a fresh entry to Heaven.

I am actually writing out, with an attempt at legibility, my play 'Miserabilia', to offer to Kegan Paul: I know it is immature, unfit for publication: but I want to see how it would strike a publisher: how it would be rejected, in what terms: don't laugh at me.

Have you read the series of 'School Board Idylls' appearing in the *Pall Mall*?[1] I can understand Charlie's ambition, if they are true.

The autumn is beautiful here, with the richest gold on the trees, and mild, melancholy air: and I walk out by the river, perfectly happy.

Will post this as it is—called away to Fearon[2]—

Yrs ever,
Lionel

Will write some day.

53

College
October 22, [1884]

Dear Badley,[3]

Before proceeding to other topics I congratulate you on your Rugby distinctions,[4] of which I was aware, tho' I never wrote at the time. Only such inducements to more frequent correspondence as I gave you were slight enough: a few worthless studies in metre, jejune and juvenile and hardly the foundations of friendship: tho' I meant them well. I have been so much occupied

---

1 James Runciman, *School Board Idylls* (1885).
2 The Headmaster. See letter 27, fn.1.
3 The first to Badley included in *Some Winchester Letters*. Although Johnson and Badley had corresponded earlier with regard to the Rugby Journal, *The Leaflet*, it is this letter that marks the point at which Badley joined the four-way correspondence. See letter 18.
4 In his final term at Rugby, Badley won both a Major and Minor Exhibition.

that I could not (I did try to find the time) manage to write to you: and now, as Editor of the *Wykehamist*, Prefect of Chapel, and sundry other intelligibilities, I am scarcely more master of my own time.

I will get rid of a confession: don't laugh: I am writing out a tragedy of mine for Kegan Paul to reject: I am about to plunge into the deep waters of printers' ink and the hell of printers' devils: merely to experience analytically an ignominious rejection of my masterpiece: oblige me by not laughing: I'll let you smile. Voilà.

I am told by indiscriminating friends that my handwriting is execrable: do you think so?

The *Wykehamist*, whose destinies I now control, is a production stereotyped by the course of the ages: it eschews literature, abhors originality, hates poetry: and Winchester loves to have it so. I can't alter it at once, tho' my leading articles avoid the usual type. Will you, if you care or have time, give me an article or poem or letter on any subject not absolutely beyond the intelligence of Wykehamists, and not quite unconnected with them? but don't trouble.

I think I enjoy two years more here dating from this September: Charlie clamours for only one year, but I can't tear myself away from a place I love so well, and where I am—excuse egoism—some kind of influence.

Winchester has, perhaps, the advantage over Rugby, of having antiquity and beauty in the midst of Philistia: of being a living spirit to commune with, in spite of Wykehamists.

I will write when I can: you know I would if I could.

Do you know at all any one here? I almost hope not, for your sake.

>Forgive illegibility and egoism;
>Yours affetly
>L.P. Johnson

54

>College
>[November 1884]

Dear Badley,

I have been guilty of great discourtesy, no less than of breach of friendship, in a silence of weeks: but I am fully occupied.

Imprimis, I will impart to you an episode, which may be fitly reckoned an important era in life: I have sent my MSS in the shape of a tragedy of 1900 lines to a publisher: and he (Kegan Paul) writes thus 'I would reject Shelley's *Cenci*, were he to offer it me as you offer your work, at my risk'. He remarks that 'no one reads poetry now: and whilst I, as an individual, accept, as a tradesman I am forced to decline.' That is success, for a seventeen year old poetaster: and it is also a far better thing, an incentive to work, to force the public into appreciation of poetry.

I send you two *Wykehamists* and make two remarks:

1. As Editor, my publisher supplies me with any number gratis: so that any account on your part is purely superfluous:

2. It is primarily a record of facts, etc, not a literary journal: wherefore, don't expect any particle of inter-

est from it.

Cambridge Wykehamists are not a striking set: Norris[1] may be worth knowing.

Are you engaged in much literary work? or how do you expend your energies? personally, I find literature an unfailing panacea against the noisome pestilences of Philistia: which is an attractive region to study for those in Paradise, if not for captives in the Temple of Dagon.[2]

I have been visiting lately the School Mission at Portsmouth: and such a visit is more suggestive than a year's dull routine: the power of the Church over chaos is striking: how it affects civilisation, is another matter. But these opportunities are very real.

I have not time now at my disposal, so, with entreaties for a letter, am

Yours
L.P. Johnson

55

College
[November 1884]

Dear Badley,

I this morning received a letter I wrote you with the *Wykehamists*, from the pleasant town of Birmingham: whither in an absent state I had sent it: so I send it to you a little out of date. You have had Russell up at

---

1 Francis Lushington Norris (1864-1945), later Bishop of North China.
2 Dagon is the biblical God of the Philistines.

Cambridge: he seems delighted with it and you all. I have no time of my own just now, with exams, etc, in prospect: but don't let that prevent your writing.

Have you ever seen Winchester? if not, I think it worth your while to see it: could you not come down to the School Concert at the end of this term, i.e., the Monday before Christmas? You'd hear not altogether bad music. I am longing for the 21st, as a young lady for her first ball, or a lover for his wedding: and from reports of it, *Ferishtah's Fancies*[1] seem likely to be a fit crown of seventy years glories.

I am due in Chapel—will try to write again—till when,

Yours
L.P. Johnson

56
To Russell

College
[November 13, 1884]

Dearest,

Just return for your letters: have burned as you wished.[2]

I can't see other than I do: but don't judge others, nor let them judge you: then Christ reigns. Peace to you.

Yrs ever
Lionel

---
1 Volume of poems by Robert Browning (1884).
2 Probably refers to letter 52 and comments made about Sayle.

57
To Sayle

College
[November 1884]

Dearest,

I know—I have been silent, forgetful of common duties: but don't blame me, who have no control over my time: I make no excuse: I have done wrong.

First then, as to your invitation: you know how my inclination answers: you know I can think of no higher pleasure: but I can't give you a definite answer, being uncertain as to other matters connected with my winter movements: so, as far as you are concerned, take my answer as a sorrowful negative: but you won't think I don't value the offer: I do.

I sent a play of mine to Kegan Paul lately: he personally wrote back most kindly:—'were Shelley to offer me *The Cenci* at my risk, I would refuse': my play he approved: the man of business said poetry was unread by the public, least of all dramas: so I must devote myself to dramas with my whole heart: I think I can do a little in that way.

You have met the Coles brothers: I have studied them both: they dislike me, but I like the younger, who is the best-hearted: the other, negative of soul, tho' more clever of mind, which is mirrorlike and all-reflective. Bennett is commonplace, good natured.[1] (I'm emulating Carlyle: God forgive me).

1 Edward Horsman Coles (1865-1948), Alfred Horsman Coles (1865-1955) and Ernest William Bennett (1866-unknown) had all just gone up to New College.

Badley must be a pleasant spirit in this world: has written me quite delightful letters, which I have answered at intervals.

You have heard Ruskin? he reads melancholy.

I have been at Landport, Portsmouth, last Sunday, among the School Mission: a strange experience: Sunday classes, talks with boys of eighteen, &c: ritualistic adorabilities: clubs, vespers, teas, all deliciously real: a veritable revelation of real work.

Rossetti's *Shelley*, 3 vols, I have just acquired:[1] a perfect work in spirit, and fascinating: I won't tell you one thought which struck me in one passage of the memoir: for it may be blasphemy.

When I don't write, don't accuse me: I have no morals, and never realise what such faults mean: I love you, I think you know: and let that stand against social shortcomings.

I would give immortality to be a music-god; to be lord of the world's pulse and nerve and spirit: aye me, I can only strive after words, with the obstacles of frivolous publics and courteously appreciative but at the same time forbidding publishers—aye me. 'Autumn wins you best':[2] and the air is keen and warm and fresh as of a deserted valley in Heaven: and I live in it happily.

Tell Frank that I literally have not time *now* to write much: you don't believe me, but it is so.

I never told you how I like 'In Memoriam': the art of it is fascinating even beyond the sense.

---

1 W. M. Rossetti (ed.), *Complete Poetical Works of Percy Bysshe Shelley: the text carefully revised with notes and a memoir*, 3 vols. (1878).
2 Robert Browning, *Paracelsus*, part 1.

Shelley is all: go where you will, the Godhead of Shelley is all: the possession of his work is heaven, and assurance of it: Shelley did not die, not die; he is alive and I shall see him as he is and cling to him, be one with him: he and Jesus are not dead, you know it: haven't they left us their divinity?

Write.

Yrs ever
Lionel

58
To Russell

College
[December 1, 1884]

Dearest, (the term is paradox)

I don't know whom I speak to now, don't know anything but that I love and love and love and would die for love of you, who are not you but all the brothers of all worlds. I seem unresponsive and cold and inattentive, but don't think ill of me: for I do love you all, who are not so distant in spirit that silence can be ominous to you. And now I have nothing to tell you at all: only I have heard the divinest music of this and all other spheres, Chopin's 'Marche Funébre' [*sic*], and it carried me high away from the earth into ecstasy, where you and all my enemies and friends were part of myself and God: I can't speak lightly of God.

Oh how ineffably mean are the world's and the hour's petty estimates—and yet they infect us. But the spirit of love is in all, and transmutes clay into air and stars—the clay and dust of daily ugliness and commonplace. Love: don't you know the meaning of universal love, the passion which is only reason and the mind of God, so unintelligible and infinite? and I am not writing now, but an infinite impulse of love which throbs through me to the torturing beautiful harmonies of Chopin's death chaunt [*sic*]. I am mad, and out of myself; myself is cold, perhaps, and undemonstrative: but you will pardon this? be secure in the thought that for me to cease from love is simply an awful death where the sweetness of death is not, but merely the agony of annihilation.

Do you doubt me? but I don't care, for the world is mine for me to love, and you are of this world of mine.

Write when you like: I don't want your letters, though I love them: for perfect love cast out fear long ago, and now lives by itself.

Yours
Lionel

59
To Russell

[December 3, 1884]

Dearest,

Alleluia! (I don't mean to be comic) I can promise, I think, two tickets: will try for three. Lady Russell, as you probably know, has kindly asked me to stay a few days: can only find time for a visit in last two or three days of holidays, not certain of that: am waiting to hear elsewhere to answer her.

No more time.

Yrs
Lionel

60

To Badley

College
December 9, [1884]

Dear (I forget your name)?

I had so completely counted upon seeing you for a few hours here, that I never thought it possible you could have to give it up: I am so sorry.

You must forgive me for only writing just these few words, because exams: are heavy upon me day and night, and I have no time for anything.

Yes, I have been reading Swinburne too, and always with unspeakable rapture: and the divinest words of him are the Cradle Songs—though possibly you won't understand that. But I have been reading *Ferishtah*, and lost in the wonder and exaltation of it: the first lyric is almost his supreme utterance for years past. Charlie's poem I have been reading—and, so far as I catch the feeling, the personal part of it, admire intensely: but I feel about his poetry, regarded as an art, that the intensity of the thought and the sense of morality, weaken the artistic side: that he, like poor Clough, mars his work with the sense of a lesson, a moral, a truth: whereas poetry has no relation to morality nor theology nor theosophy, but is for itself: one verse of the 'Blessed Damozel' is to me worth the whole of 'Dipsychus': do you feel that? Matthew Arnold writes no poetry now, and wrote much false poetry, by this failure to define the working of art.

Have you got the *Wykehamist*? an amusing instance of the failure to grasp the meaning poetry is given me by the public criticisms on the verse therein contained, some mine, some Oxford friends': all of the same unreal stamp, all with some element of strangeness, all with art as their principle: the public here is laughing consumedly—so am I. But Charlie's book is a true poem.

Do you know Robert Buchanan's poetry?

Must turn to the plague at Athens—eheu.

Yours ever
Lionel

61

Rhual, N. Wales
December 24, [1884]

Dear Jack,

Thanks for the sight again of your handwriting. How I wish I was with you at Tenby, a place which is almost an ideal of my first memories: I was there for a year at the age of five and again, at the age of nine: and to this day St Catharine's Rock, Lundy, etc, are a kind of fairy dream. As you see, I am in the wilds of Wales, in frost and snow: mainly reading, and trying to write: another play, if possible: but I can't get it clear in my head. If only you could have come to Winchester: I think you would have liked the place, if not the people. But you must come in the summer, when nothing on earth is more beautiful than the wide, gray downs panting under a burning sky.

Russell may be coming to stay with me soon, to make the acquaintance of my people—I don't altogether know the probable result.

The sea is the most wonderful thing in the world—I remember a wreck off Lundy, years ago, and the lifeboat, and a great storm and midnight—and myself, a terrified child, at the window, watching it all as a play or a poem of Victor Hugo—had I known Hugo then.

Write to me when you feel inclined—you don't know the delight of letters from a friend, even when we have never met—a strange fascination in the idea: but I want your 'likeness', and must have it—pardon my importunacy.

Christmas in Wales is so unfamiliar to me, some way: but I always love the idea of Xmas, tho' not as the Xtians about me. 'Peace on earth, good will' is the best definition of Brotherhood of Shelley's type.

Write.

Yrs ever
Lionel

62

Rhual
Xmas Eve [1884]

Dearest Frank,

Am at last settled down. Can you come here from the 1st to the 8th, or from the 9th to the 13th?

Circumstances limit the possible time to one of those two periods. Let me know when you can if you think it worth while to come any distance for such a length of time: if you will come, tell me when and by what train from where—that you may be met at Mold. No more now,

Peace on earth.

Yours
Lionel

63
To Russell

Rhual
[December 26, 1884]

Dearest,

Your letter was the vaguest thing I ever read: but, finally, we can only receive you between the 1st and 8th: so, will you come on the 1st, leave on the 7th, or come on the 3rd (my people wouldn't understand the 4th, which is Sunday!) and leave on the 7th? Choose as suits you: I only hint that three days is not long, if you can spare more. Let me know soon.

Pardon abruptness—I am in hurry.

What a glorious man Thomson was, or is: his poem on Shelley is the most Shelleyan thing I know. I can't thank you enough for the book, doubly sacred.

Yours
Lionel

I hope I've made myself clear: but I hate practicalities.

64
To Russell

Rhual
[December 28, 1884]

Dearest,

Could you, without inconvenience, manage to come by an earlier train, e.g. the 2.30 (or something like it) from Chester? some of us dine some way off that night, and dinner is, I believe, earlier than usual: and the Mold trains are always late and few and far between. The 2nd will do perfectly: I wish we could keep you beyond the 7th, but I am afraid we can't.

Yours is haste,
Lionel

The 6.22 will do, if you are unable to find anything else.

65

Rhual
[December 29, 1884]

Dear Jack,

It seems so altogether strange, all this unconventional friendship of strangers, and the something higher than friendship crowning our friendship. I can imagine no more beautiful happiness than to walk with you by the sea in the winter and the cold fresh breath of winds and waves: yet it was merely a fancy of loveliness, beyond my power to realize in act now: we shall we see each other some day, though not at Tenby. I am waiting for your 'graven image' in impatience: pardon me the confession—it is a 'graven image' that I must worship, having but once glanced at it: you see, I can say in absence what your presence might check. And you too ask me for my image: which does not exist, except at the age of ten or thereabouts: well, when it has an existence, which will be in a few weeks, I will send it to you: but it will be absolutely devoid of attractiveness.

My miserable play is now being copied into legible MS by the loving labour of a cousin, the only member of my family to whom I can really disclose myself: when it is ready, I shall send it the round of the publishers: by the time it returns to me like Noah's dove, my self-conceit will, let us hope, have been disillusioned.

Russell comes to us on the 2nd, for a few days: which will be a break upon the monotony of spiritual solitude.

You must come to Winchester some day, and alone: besides the beautiful divinity of the place, I think Winchester should be our place of meeting—when you can, do come: though Cambridge and Tenby and Dudley are alike far away.

Have you anywhere in your possession some infinitely valueless rhymes of mine, which I cruelly foisted upon you, the unknown editor of a few months ago? if so, don't keep them—in the light of somewhat increased powers of self criticism, if not of execution, they show so worthless that they cannot really be an integral part of me.

Let me enjoy something of the work of your hands, whether poetry of words or design: I shall regard it as a sign that after all you are not merely attracted by the unreal portraits of me my friends may have given you, nor merely are studying me with interest: but that you can accept somewhat of me for its own sake so far as you can see it.

I hardly know why I am writing in this way: perhaps it comes from long staring out at great soft ridges of misty hills, with gray clouds about them, and flashes of white snow upon them: a sense of a great melancholy indifference to the world and its life: I don't know.

Will you, when you write to me, analyze your conception of Charley, as a human soul? I will not try to describe my sensations—for they are sensations more than ideas—of him: but he is at least very strange, and, though loveable to the uttermost, at times almost unacceptable.

Do you know in your own mind, or heart, what your after life is to be? and have you ever thought it possible that you should become a priest, as I hope to become?

Is there not at Tenby a headland or cape called Gilter or Gilder Point? I have a dim memory of it as the limit of a childish walk starting from St. Katharine's rock: and it is quite clear to me still in imagination.

'Oh to be at Tenby
Now that you are there!'[1]

but I can't. Vale.
Yours
Lionel

---

1 Robert Browning, 'Home Thoughts, from Abroad' (1845), 'Oh, to be in England / Now that April's here'.

66
To Sayle

Rhual
[January 1885][1]

Dearest,

I am bearing your cross, and you have my thanks for it. That you have not heard from me again is not to be attributed to carelessness, but to an entire want of time.

The world is very amusing. Frank is with us, tasting the quality of Philistia: he rather seems to endure it, and reproaches me with intentional cruelty towards my people—a strange side of the matter.

Jack has been most kind in the way of letters, and we think we know each other, however absurd a supposition for two human souls. At least, he does not appear cold; nor offensively hysterical; as men are apt to show themselves.

Why is it that men would be intolerably dull without religion to discuss? you see, religion is the ideal platitude in personal intercourse: and it sickens me inexpressibly. There is more delight in the structure of a sonnet or villanelle, the cadence of a verse, than in heavy analysis of a foggy soul; Rossetti is the infinite Hyperion, and Clough an ineffable Satyr with the music of Beddoes' 'frog-voice'.[2]

---

1 This letter, dated by Russell, can be more accurately dated by Russell's visit to Rhual, 2-7 January (see letter 64).
2 Beddoes, 'Song by Isbrand' (1851), 'Squats on a toad-stool

It is hard to be natural, and to know oneself: I am never certain that I don't hate my friends: if I did, there would be no difference from loving them: things are so inconceivably little. Silence is the best speech: silence is an existence, but speech an impotence and a mockery.

I verily believe that the dearth of all high literature, and the sterility of all social happiness, is due to the cursed spirit of religious gossip, the breath of rotten philosophies. Shelley, whom we worship, was content with love for his God, faith and hope for his politics; he read Shakespeare, and cared nothing for Herbert Spencer: the outcome, pure divinity of literature. But you wretched pseudo Athenians babble over your Clough and your religion, and would 'boggle at' the first canto of the Faery Queen.

I won't continue: I feel angry and rude.

In love,
Lionel.

67
To Badley

College
[c. 21 January, 1885][1]

Dearest

Your last letter reached me at Pembroke Lodge, where I have spent the last few days before coming back to the home of my heart. And now I feel far too weary with wayfaring to write connectedly. Meanwhile

---

under a tree / A bodiless childfull of life in the gloom / Crying with frog voice, "What shall I be?"'
1 Dated by the first day of term which was 21 January.

you are back at Cambridge: and I wait and long for your visible appearing, immediately, in image: and love only knows when, in reality. I think I shall not die yet, that I shall waste on into old age and memories of a beautiful life: for life is meaningless without beauty, and everything is or becomes at need, beautiful.

You will forgive this wearisomeness of mine: I am not writing you a letter, merely saying things. Chiefly, that parting and absence are the bitterest of experiences: that to be away from the sphere and hourly contact of one whom we love is a sword that pierces to the death of the body and the utter pain of the soul: and you, whose face alone I know, and others whom you do not know—all these I have not with me, or have left elsewhere: and I want to speak or sing and die rather than know that these are in a strange land where strangers to me love them: for love is sinful even to the sin of jealousy. 'This unintelligible world';[1] and we in the midst of it.

Write to me, speak to me anyhow: and let me have your face and fashion with me;

Yours
Lionel

68
To Badley

[January 1885]

Dearest

I am writing to you face to face at last, in sight of

---

[1] Wordsworth, 'Lines Composed a Few Miles Above Tintern Abbey' (1798).

you, to you: you must imagine my gratitude: I am grateful.

As to myself, I have not forgotten my promise: but the photographer declines to do anything until the sun shines, being an ancient and conservative man: at present and, to all appearances, into das [*sic*] Ewigkeit,[1] the sun is dead behind gray clouds. But I will send myself, though I don't know when.

I hardly know now what to say to you: words are very easy things, and not very expressive.

Marchant[2] I know by sight imperfectly, have never spoken to or come across, socially or other how: he never attracted me, and probably knows nothing of me worth knowing—if that is not a truism to say of any one.

Why is Charley in a state of meaningless wrath and sorrow against me? for his last letters are entirely unfathomable—he was merely mystic and maudlin alternately: and now I seem to have lost my self-complacency, at the thought of it. But I think nothing is wrong.

How work wastes life: the scholarship and pedantry and dustiness of learning are strangely cramping to the imagination: a chapter of philology unfits me by the blank horror of it, to write a line of verse for a week.

Don't be annoyed or worse if I don't write often: I am not too well in body just now, and find an effort where there should be none.

---

1 'die Ewigkeit': Eternity.
2 Possibly John Marchant (1868-unknown), Commoner at Winchester from autumn 1883.

You cannot understand the extent of your gift of yourself—to me it means worlds of memory and association: I can turn to you now as to a Madonna. But you will write when you can: a word, as a look from passing eyes in the street, is a breath of love to be stored up: and the more I live and the more nearly I know the few true friends I love, the more precious becomes the gift of any least word. To one living alone, the striking of a single chord of music is a real part of Heaven. Don't think me cold, if I don't write—

Yours
Lionel

69
To Sayle

[January 1885]

Why is it, dearest, that you are always restless as to other people's states of mind, always imagining strange emotions for them? From your letter I gather that you are angry and resentful with me: or that you suppose me to be so with you: and so I am to atone for your forcible imagination by desisting to wear a beautiful gift of you to me: and you are entirely amusing in every way. Because I do not write, or do not seem to sympathise, or do not share your emotions,—hinc illae lachrimae;[1] unreasonably. Yet, all manifestation of nature and human souls at work is pleasing: you are always the same to me: I will always love your Ich—in-

---

1 Hence those tears.

terpret as you may. Pardon me my neglect in retaining 'To my brethren': you know I will send it you: but it is so far mine that I forget its real ownership: I will send tomorrow. Your character is a thing that cannot suffer in my eyes: it may change and shift and develop: so I can study it and be happy with it and be emotional at the same time. Let me know what you mean: and, if you truly feel unable to care about me—you won't be the first or last—then I shall be impassive as before: 'nothing in Heaven can be Greater than pain'.

Do you comprehend me? you and Frank and Jack—oh you can never really leave me or like me: I can leave you and love you. Is this over much oracular? at least it is truth.

If you are not at peace with me and all men, 'look up in perfect silence at the stars'.[1]

Yours
Whether I will or no
Lionel

70
To Badley

College
[January 23, 1885]

Dearest

For two reasons—both none of my making—fate is against us. First, I am—and feel likely to remain—too ill to do any thing—merely the weariness of work

---

1 Walt Whitman, 'When I Heard the Learn'd Astronomer' (1865), 'Look'd up in perfect silence at the stars'.

prostrating me—secondly, some of my people will be here, taking up more of my time than is compatible with my duties of love to you. Ah Jack, how hard it is—

> Yours in love
> Lionel

71

> College
> [February 8, 1885]

Dear Frank

I have not written to you for years, I think: but you know I am lazy at home and busy here—and letters fall to the ground.

Lady Russell[1] was very kind and very averse to my whole attitude of mind—and delighted me by denouncing 'you young men who are full of "doing good to others" and none to yourself'. But she was extremely suggestive—if that doesn't sound patronizing.

I have heard from Charlie, and he was full of Roberts,[2] whom he was ecstatic over: otherwise he was oracular and rather suspicious. But Jack I seem to know more and more: his photo I never have out of my sight, through sheer delight in its beauty.

---

1 Russell replaces 'Lady Russell' with 'Your Aunt' in *Some Winchester Letters*, suggesting Johnson refers to Lady Agatha (letter 48, fn.2) not Russell's grandmother, Lady John.
2 Herbert Ainslie Roberts (1864-1932) was at Cambridge with Badley. Sayle noted in his diary that Roberts gave him a copy of William Morris' *The Life and Death of Jason* (1867), presumably as a birthday gift, in January 1885.

Winchester is all as usual, and I am settled down to work. I have shouted myself hoarse in Debating Society in denouncing vivisection, alone, against a horde of flippantly clever utilitarian sciolists who 'prated of humanity' and the value of life. The Second Master last Sunday preached us a splendid sermon, full of really striking thought, perfect Buddhism and high spirituality: a glorious sermon, delivered almost as well.[1] Tonight, Spooner of New College: with whom I dine at Fearon's.[2] Money-Kyrle[3] is my colleague in the editorship, at my special request: he is quite surprisingly and pleasingly capable. As you see, faith is in my family a large element of belief: my father with his 'omnipotent', my mother with her churchism—see what faith is. I feel rather bitter in temper, as though selfishness were really more strong than love: it never is. But I seem lonely, even with the many I love, you and those whom you know in common with me, and a few you don't know—lonely altogether by my own fault. My nature is not deeply sympathetic, but deeply impressionable. I am hard.

Forgive my egoism; and write sometimes.

Yours
Lionel.

---

1 In consequence of Johnson's enthusiasm for the sermon and Russell's fondness for George Richardson, Russell inserted an extract from the sermon after this letter in *Some Winchester Letters*.
2 Spooner identified letter 14, fn.4; Fearon in letter 27, fn.1.
3 Rowland Tracy Ashe Money-Kyrle (1866-1928), Archdeacon of Hereford from 1923.

72
To Russell

College
[February 26, 1885]

Dearest

Excuse a hurried scrawl. I shld have written, I know—but work is pressing: I have worlds to say, when I do write—which will be soon. Shall see the Daker tomorrow.

Write soon.

Yrs ever in love,
Lionel.

73
To Sayle

College
[February-March 1885][1]

Dearest

You have not heard from me lately, nor have I from you: that means very little. And even now that I am breaking a happy silence, it is mainly for practical purposes.

You once mentioned a picture—whether engraving, etching, &c., I don't know—of Shelley in your possession; can you tell me where I can get a portrait of him not unworthy of his name? I have hunted all

---

1 Incorrectly sequenced by Russell who dated it 15 June 1884. Reference to the receipt of Badley's photo and Johnson's meeting with Spooner of New College place it more accurately as following letter 69 (January 1885) and the request for Shelley's photo as preceding letter 74 (9 March 1885).

London, and can't light upon what I want. It is for a cousin who almost literally prays to Shelley, having lost all her other Gods. Could you help me here? Also, I will send you 'To My Brethren' at once: and you must not be more than reasonably angry with me for having detained your property. Badley's face I now possess, and his letters: of all the good your friendship has been to me, his friendship and brotherhood are the best. And that is high praise. What kind of being is Richards[1] of the *Leaflet*, with whom I have interchanged a letter or two and sent him some verses? he seems very much in earnest.

I have met Spooner of New College here: he talked omnisciently of all of you: you in especial he analysed with the intensest air of certainty. A fearless man in what he says.

You will write and let me have an answer to my question?

Ever yours
L

74
To Sayle

College
[March 9, 1885]

Dearest

Your Shelley photo I knew without possessing: in my eyes it has greater charm than the engraved por-

---

1 George Chatterton Richards (1867-1951), classical scholar and Canon of Durham, then still at Rugby, went up to Balliol in 1885.

traits. Thank you. As I thought, a large portrait of any kind is not attainable: one must remain without—tho' it is hard. The Rossetti portrait after Stothard is undoubtedly preferable to Miss Curran's in Buxton Forman—worlds more beautiful to me: but association with Stothard of Shelley is heartrending to a lover of Blake.[1] Your photograph has the most personal expression of any presentments of Shelley know to me. What of Henn?[2] whom I have heard a certain amount from Frank.

Also Richards of the *Leaflet*—he has written to me very pleasantly, and seems attractive.

Fillingham appears to have set the world or microcosm of Oxford in an uproar—is he any way worth notice? he displays all the symptoms of Protestantism run mad and hydrophobic—as Faulkner in an other extreme.[3] You Oxford people don't strike me as very sane on most points; you are morbidly self-conscious and not over civilized; and largely Philistine. At least,

---

1 Johnson refers to two portraits of Shelley: an engraving in vol. 1 of W. M. Rossetti's edition of the poems (see letter 57), and an engraving after the portrait by Amelia Curran in vol. 1 of Henry Buxton-Forman (ed.), *The Prose Works of Percy Bysshe Shelley*, 5 vols. (1880). He may be confusing Thomas Stothard (1755-1834) with George J. Stodart (unknown-1884).
2 Percy Umfreville Henn (1865-1955) of Worcester College, later an educationalist and Headmaster of Guildford Grammar School, Western Australia.
3 Robert Charles Fillingham (1861-1908), then an undergraduate at Merton College, and Charles Joseph Faulkner (1833-92), a mathematics master at University College. Both were politically active at this time in opposite camps: Faulker as a friend and associate of William Morris (see also letter 10) and Fillingham as a member of the newly established university habitation of the Primrose League.

you cannot endure passive existence and enjoyment.

Is Farrar[1] saying things worth hearing? beyond *Eternal Hope*, I have an aesthetic dislike to him—too much early Christian martyr about him.

I am very much occupied with work of multifarious nature: so can write very seldom. Let me hear from you when you feel inclined.

With much thanks.

Yrs,
L.

75
To Russell

College
[March 15, 1885]

Dearest

I am not now writing at any length: but merely a few words to satisfy your rapacity. Imprimis, the Convocation catastrophe has depressed me: your public mind—if you have one—is rotten.

I am revelling in Pater's book: full of the most perfect literary quality, and infinitely wise and true and beautiful.[2]

I have not thanked you for your flowers: molte grazie. I was at St. John's lately, and heard the Daker on almsgiving—not even his usual spiritual irony, but

---

1 Dean Frederick William Farrar (1831-1903), Archdeacon of Westminster at this time.
2 Walter Pater, *Marius the Epicurean: his Sensations and Ideas* (1885).

rather a stinging satire throughout, delivered in his most contemptuous voice: it was of M. Arnold's and Swinburne's finest quality in righteous scorn. Hélas, how terrible it is γηράσκειν![1] I am eighteen years today, I wish I were ten younger: do you know anything of a leading pessimist German philosopher, by name von Hartmann? his final solution is instantaneous suicide of the race by an act prompted by pure reason, attained after a period of education. Whitman is individual, yes, but so is God, and all of us are individual: the supreme aim is to individualize the universe into a myriad unity of individuals: see Blake, whom study well.

The *Wykehamist* is none of my work this time. I will write more when I have time—but I have work, and with me it must be done, sorely against the grain.

Yrs ever
Lionel

76
To Sayle

Rhual
[April 1885][2]

My dearest,

I have much that I should like to say to you, but I cannot at all. Your flowers were whole worlds of delight to me all the night—and Mrs. Richardson then had them—and I thank you in silence, as my

---

1 Gēraskein, to grow old.
2 Russell incorrectly sequenced and dated this letter 23 December 1884. It is more accurately dated by the reference to Johnson's birthday flowers and Johnson being in Rhual for the Easter vacation which began on 1 April.

way is. Speech is to me almost impossible together with bodily presence—speech is weak and shame-faced—but in absence words are all things. 'Vicisti et vivimus' conquered, yet alive—is our motto—from an old legend of the Scotch border when we were a clan of Johnstones—I like it, for it means so much in different ways.

I hardly know what my movements will be now—all is unsettled here: at least I am resting, and trying to write poetry. Jack's face is simply haunting: from one glance at its copy, I remember each portion of it, each expression of eyes and mouth—I must see him some day.

Through all the changes and chances of life, I think one must be happy, with men and nature round one: I have passed through London and now write looking over wild Welsh hills—and my mind is the same, always full of beautiful happiness—life is very worth living, and death leads to another.

If you write within a week, at all events, I shall be here—so write, if just to tell me that you forgive me my cold silence—you know what it meant.

Yours ever
Lionel

77
To Russell

Rhual
[April 6, 1885]

Dearest

I have for months, I think, disregarded you entirely in spite of my own conscience and your protests: and now I am making slight amends. Yes, I am anticipating the being with you on the 18th. Shortly after you had left Winchester with Henn, I heard from him: a most kindly letter, written with the same affection and the same beautiful calligraphy that all you people affect: and I answered him, though so singularly destitute of both those good qualities. At present I am recovering from the effects of experiencing the lovely Passion Week in Mold, in a cold, shivering air, with no smallest savour of beautiful Catholicism to make the divinity of the Passion a delight: dull, cheerless routine of unimpassioned, uninspired services; no light and colour and solemnity of ritual: and my soul is too weak to live without these. You are, I think, at Winchester, the beautiful city whom I never love so well as when I am in Mold. I am half happy here, with a careful selection of treasure in the way of literature: I have with me Blake, Christina Rossetti, Walt Whitman, a little beautiful modern minor poetry (notably one O'Shaughnessy, unknown, I should guess, to you), *Belinda* by Rhoda Broughton: and the perfection of beautiful literature, Pater's *Marius*: a revelation of wonderful beauty and delight: a book to love and worship: a good book. So I find life pleasant, but for this chilly April: and I am writing little songs, etc. as a relief from the pressures of school work. The future never is a thing that I like to speculate about: life for the moment seems right now, the closer that I approach to the days of decision: I simply hate the days for flying past so speedily. When the endless region of faith and doubt is once entered, life becomes weary of itself: and to remain without that land, contented with the colours of a rainbow and a curtain, the sound of a storm and a sonata, appears the higher, more dignified way. But life is very difficult always and everyway. And this philosophy or want of it is catholic: it allows me to delight in the irreverent cleverness of Orange[1] and the boisterous indifference of—well, my brother. And, as you see, it permits me to hold monologues by way of writing letters. Perhaps you know better than I what may be the reason: but I find letter writing impossible now: assuredly not for the simple reason of 'nothing to say': nor from indifference: is it a prosaic and gross laziness?

Yrs in love
Lionel

I enclose a note from my mother.

I don't know where you are staying: write before the 18th.

78
To Badley

Rhual
[April 24, 1885]

Dearest Jack

Don't think I have forgotten you, for I have never forgotten you: but I have sinned by silence: you will forgive me.

I have been at Oxford, in a pure ecstasy of delight

---

[1] Hugh William Orange (1866-1956), later an educationalist and schools inspector.

at the communion of Saints there vouchsafed.[1] I will write tomorrow: but don't forget me. I have been photographed, and will send myself when ready.

With all love
Yours
Lionel.

79
To Badley

Rhual[2]
[April 25, 1885][3]

Dearest Jack

My apology and humble appeal for restoration into full communion with you once more I performed yesterday: and now I write in confidence and in trust. Since last I heard from you—how long ago that seems!—I have been intensely interested in life in many ways—and my philosophy or systematic want of it has received its final perfection in the few days lately lived at Oxford. Not the beautiful spell and associations—not the thought and idea of the holy and eternal city—rather the personal delight and fascination of contact with free life and free love: the sense of fellowship has

---

1 Johnson visited Oxford on 18 Apr 1885 and was back in Winchester when this was written.
2 Johnson does not cross this through on the original, but the letter admits to being written from College.
3 Russell incorrectly dated this letter 1884. It is more accurately dated by Johnson's visit to Oxford and even more specifically by his reference to his restoration of communion with Badley on the previous day in letter 78.

seized hold upon me. By nature unfamiliar enough and unemotional, still the close intimacy of those whom I can feel for in common, has been a dreamy revelation of happiness. Charlie, Frank, Osman, Henn, and two others whom you may know, Thynne and Jepson—these men are real in themselves, to love or to ignore:[1] and the common union of these in showing me the love which I can never externally seem to appreciate and return, is a divine thing and a solution of many fitful doubts and longings. Mere life, mere life, that is enough: not the thought alone, not the various work, not the pleasures alone: but the mere reality of common existence. That solves all the questions: is it possible to hate or be jealous, to teach or to inspire, when I can reject no one and no thing? brotherhood is God.

And you—are you able to look upon the world with calmness, or are you yet suffering in the body? let me have some knowledge of you: don't distrust me: I have not seen you, but what of that, when love is the daily air and common sun of all lives? Back at Winchester, beautiful with growing leaves and warm breath of April and promise of full summer perfection: yet even so, and amid the work of school life, and the employments of my own personal life, there is a void and a vacant space: loneliness is a little lonely at times—and I am lonely here, so far as personal love is

---

1 At Oxford, Johnson was introduced to Russell and Sayle's friends: Herbert Edward Osman Edwards (1864-1936) of Merton College, later an author and Japanese translator; Henn—see letter 74, fn.2; John Alexander Roger (Ion) Thynne (1863-1914) of New College, sent down in 1886 for 'having lived outside college for two terms without permission'; Edgar Alfred Jepson (1863-1938) of Balliol, later a prolific popular author.

involved: pleasant friendship, interest—these I have, but I want more. Osman and Henn are very loveable: both utterly kind to me, a stranger: and both with the sense of natural humour and natural laughter which preserves love from falling into distorted jealousy and selfishness—ah, how unspeakably grateful I must be to you all, you who without the pretext of friendship, go further and will make me happy in the warmth of your love—if that is not a dream, a passing thought born in upon my loneliness. I can only write in this way: I want to sing, to be intoxicated in delight of life: I have lived, and might die in the truth of that. But now future fortunes and the cares of future responsibilities, all the burden of ignorant expectancy, fall away: I am alive, and strong in the thought of that life. And all this, from a few hours with a few human beings. Write to me before very long, before my dream dies—before I am cold again and irresponsive and dull. At present I am happy. Myself shall be with you soon—not ready yet.[1]

In real love
Yours
Lionel.

80
To Sayle

[April 1885]

Dearest

    'Après tant de jours—'[2] shall I continue the quo-

1 Johnson refers to his promised photograph.
2 After so many days. The quote is from a French song by Swinburne, included in his tragedies *Chastelard* (1865) and *Mary*

tation?—your handwriting again comes to console me, who am never above consolation, despite my Epicurean sloth: at last. And I was made supremely happy yesterday with a letter from Jack, utterly full of loving kindness—and the sun is shining brightly, if somewhat coldly. You were very good to me at Oxford: and marvellously refused to be frozen and chilled by the iciness of my calm self-sufficing—for which I thank you. As for 'Words of Parting', written in roundel form and with the peculiar 'melancholy grace' of youthful meditation—I read them now for the first time—can tell you nothing of them, except that I can feel sympathy with their tone: and I have an unverifiable kind of certainty that you are yourself the author—quae si ita sint,[1] the remainder will be verily welcome—or if you still maintain the attitude of ignorance, the specimen I have is enough to create a desire to know the whole—there is nothing on earth—perhaps not even music, not even painting—of equal divinity with a single line of pure word-music, a single thought caught from passing emotions and changing aspects, and fashioned into the beauty of a phrase—there is nothing equally sovereign with poetry. All things must be everlastingly right, and so the worlds are ordered by the law of unchecked license which sees and has no bounds: life is justified by its every possibility of action or negation—that is all. Why do I take delight in the coarsest expressions of life, and also take delight in the colourless purities and statuesque innocence of a moral law and a mild instinct? why, whilst with you all lately, have I never heard one

---

Stuart (1877).
1 If it is so.

word repulsive to my humanity? wonder and laughter and appreciation and enthusiasm and disbelief—all these are natural, but never the cold air of a shuddering superiority, never the sweet contempt of an instructive pity. Frank inwardly wails over me; 'quantum mutatus!' but no, not changed from a lofty pedestal of aspiration to the vulgar level of cowardly acquiescence: rather the same to the end, shifting and multifariously tolerant. Is there this higher life men talk of? is there this lower they deprecate so blatantly? I thought that Jesus put that lie to flight. In struggle and hard contest and opposing ways, where is your light, unless it be in the love of all things human and inhuman? love is a reality, after all: at least it is possible and always beautiful. I may yet one day in the future before me, waste away in the ecstatic agony of aspiration and self-denial: I may yet writhe away to the outer darkness on the shuddering horror of a passion-consumed body: meanwhile I am alive in the summer heat and flowers, and can laugh at the prospect of either melodrama. Does this preclude seriousness and 'Ernsthaft' generally?[1] well, I find that a moral laissez-faire combined with a practical, working, love and affection or tolerance of my brothers, makes my life not ignoble in my sight. I will grant you sin and the blessedness of piety and the superior thrill of self satisfaction arising therefrom: what then? these things may be, but I also see such other matters as misery and Philistinism and hypocrisy and content—and all these varieties become mingled again into the coloured world I live in—I cannot distinguish except by an uncongen-

---

1 Serious. 'Ernsthaft' is an adjective, but Johnson uses it here as a noun.

ial effort of analysis. Perhaps this is the unscientific, unexact labyrinth of verbal plausibilities? very likely you are right: again, what of that? my object is to live as I see life possible: not to set up theories. I hate a settled opinion on matters which seem to me to exist only to be debated. That Catullus is the truest Roman poet: that Knox Little is the greatest English orator: that Chopin's Funeral March is higher than the Eroica March: these definite views I hold, and will defend: but that it is wrong to be immoral, wrong to be infidel, wrong to be insincere—the very words have no meaning to me. I know what is meant by them—but that meaning is meaningless to me. My emotions refuse to answer such platitudes, paradoxes, truths, lies, theses, axioms—call them what you will. None the more do I say that it is right to speak the truth, to go to Church, to refrain from adultery: equally here I do not know what to say to these collocations of words. Shallow and low and unoriginal—oh yes, if you will. Have I bored you enough with my apologia? forgive me: I have been reading Blake—always an emotional rapture—and Blake has a strong common sense—which may have proved infectious. Every new specimen of the potter's power over the clay of the world impels me to the belief: the watching of a human face with its strange power of impressing you as a sacred and mysterious shrine of hidden and self contained passions: the mere act of hearing a voice, observing a gesture, feeling a form not your own near you: the thought that there are others like yourself, if you could but act upon that knowledge:— all this is the proof and sign of the faith to which I think my practice and conduct clung before my senses and mind were impressed with its very truth. I consider now, writing—thank God—alone, how many faces I have known of late, and how much each face has shewn me. Apart from these esoteric, rhapsodical aspects of my late visit, I think of Osman—Henn—Thynne—Jepson—Fillingham—Roberts—Walker—Kelsall—all practically unknown to me before:[1] and then what a rush of memory and suggestion! what a strange vision of casual thoughts and sensations! and that, not from any high moments of elevation, from no high-strung impulses: merely from an hour's random talk, a breakfast, a stroll, a Chapel service, and thus a thousand little things tend to the same end: I know because I feel, that these effects are now a part of me, actual and interwoven. So life becomes a liturgy sung to the Gods of our most beautiful imagination. You now—do you think that you are merely a friend whom I have talked with, walked with, written to, experienced? oh no, not that: you are closer than that, you are a thought of love and hours of memory and a part of my life: and so our union is closer than our personal intercourse could make it. This may have a cold, repulsive side to it in your eyes: it may not sound like the loves of historical lovers, nor the companionship of historical friends: but it is absolutely literal and exact. True, your worst hatred and contempt poured upon me could not alter my sensations towards you: they would merely vary them in a new direction: but do you not see a transcendent possibility of faith-

---

[1] In addition to those identified in letter 79 are Charles Henry Roberts (1865-1959) of Balliol, later MP for Lincoln; John Edward Kelsall (1864-1924) of Balliol who became a cleric; and possibly James Walker (1864-unknown) of Balliol, future British diplomat. Fillingham identified letter 74, fn.3.

ful brotherhood and love in that creed? Surely, whilst we live our hours, let us be at peace: for there is peace in the tumultuous thunder of antiphonal music, and the supremacy of rapturous peace in the glories of a calm sun moving with quiet heat: no peace in Exeter Hall, no peace in the *Principles of Polit: Econ:* none in the pity of false Christians.[1] Are you still for morality and convention? then my love, such as it is to you, will merely change form a little: for you will still be the same, still a separate and unknowable personality, as we are all separate and unknowable. A 'damned nuisance' is a bad definition of life: Heine is nearer the facts with his definition of his poetry: so, applying that to life, I think of life as 'a divine plaything'. Quaint, the thought that I don't know nor care to know, whence my life has reached me—and why I can write of myself as an entity apart from my life. Strange and laughable, these stray thoughts: not real agonies of earnest endeavour, but fragments of curious music, experiments of rococo metres: curious work of fancy—suggesting John of Patmos and Jerusalem, Lucian, Swedenborg: and therefore pleasant and profitable: meanwhile, perhaps I have a headache or can help a brother: a practical solution of these cases is more within my scope. But this is old and natural enough.

If you were to die soon, what should I experience, what sensation? well, besides the common and pathetic kind of physical shock, would not all the past year

---

[1] Exeter Hall was large meeting house on the Strand in London, a venue for religious and philanthropic meetings and lectures and home to the YMCA; *Principles of Political Philosophy* was by Mill (1848).

or so become changed to me, and the colour of the future shaded curiously? old trains of ideas, remembrances and associations would flock about me—it would drift into a Rossettian sonnet—and fly across the summer light and mingle with organ tones and flash from gleaming streams and sigh up from flowers; all the air would become a melancholy, which would cling and melt and hang; and at last always I should keep the sense of loss and a pure delight of real sorrow: a phrase in a book, a sudden aspect of the sky, might represent a part of your impressions upon me now: and you would live for me so, I should be enriched by the pity of it. Ah, do you think this an affectation, or a cruelty? to me it has a beautiful force and persistence. And when I die, even then the same pleasure of impression will be with me: for all else is uncertain. My Catholic Saints and seraphs tell me this, and I knew it before I knew them: Browning, Blake, Swinburne, Rossetti, Hugo, Whitman, Pater, Catullus, Chopin, and many more: all pass through the world with holy indifference and tolerant favour on their lips, the sun of righteousness in their eyes, for the healing of the nations.

Believe me capable of what you will: suspect me, distrust me, despise me (an echo from afar of Hugo and Josiane):[1] but never hate me, never cast me away. You don't know how far I am insincere, rhetorical, hollow, dull, affected, shallow: and you don't know how far I am simple and actual. At least my love is a strangely persistent passion. I am very thankful to you

---

[1] La Duchesse Josiane, a character in Hugo's novel *The Man Who Laughs* (1869).

all for your kindness: according to my lights, that is inevitable.

My work this term is of especial importance to me from a gross and practical point of view: so don't look for many letters. I feel an impulse to recite a creed this evening. Will you respond an Amen?

My love to any who may be affected by it, and always to you.

Lionel.

81
To Russell

[College
April 24, 1885]

Dearest

Having at last settled down to the life which at last seems to me the peculiar state God has been pleased to call me to—the life of placid irritation and fascinating isolation—I can write from a natural attitude. Verily, there are many things ready for the saying: as you know by experience, I never have been externally emotional nor receptive—I slip away into cold conceit or dull passivity. But I have certainly reason to be emotional now: *me voilà* in Philistia, and behind me is the kindly light of Israel. I am as grateful as my nature allows to you all: I know by the personal standard of my impressions that I have been unusually happy with you—I gave you no reason for thinking so: but ça va. The return to this lonely haunt of dullness is a positive discomfort, only capable of yielding the delight of enforced contrast: well, I thank you all.

There are now ~~nine~~ ten names at Oxford which in various degrees and manners are memorable to me: they have entwined themselves with strange thoughts and beautiful faces and holy books: a real addition to my sensuous-perceptive memory-power (German) has been given by the experiences of a few days. Pessimism is a glorious spell, if it has made me think the world as good for a moment as it could be. I have incurred the penalty of Faust: I have said the inevitable words to so many moments of so many hours. Gratitude sits awkwardly upon me: it produces a gasping incoherence—you will understand.

Ach, the loneliness here, the agonizing stupidity of these banal Christians about me: the childish ignorance and the childish annoyance of this healthy and well-meaning society—it is not my fault that I can simply fall back upon sense and impression as antidotes and opiates: you see, there is no actuality of real life, that I should hate it or mingle with it or study it: merely the scholastic-pious and the athletic-ear-splitting factions. 'So I am what I am, and what you shun,' to quote O'Shaughnessy. Mean[while] I must work, work, drive myself mad with it.

Henn foolishly insisted upon carrying away some of my sins of commission in the way of verse: the quasi-dramatic sketch is uninteresting except to me as an experiment in form and metre and music: but I also gave him a few lyrics I wrote a few days before coming to you: will you see what you can make of them? perhaps I may confess that most of them are addressed to a man here in Junior Part, a Commoner, whom I have scarcely spoken to: but whom I cannot forget: and who therefore has not yet come back—weh mis daruber.[1] The Winchester people, the authorities, receive me with their customary show of interest: so that your latitudinarian impostor in priest's clothing has evoked his flattering recollection of me from his own sense of irresponsible vexatiousness—for which may the Sanctus Spiritus reward him. Acting upon your suggestion, I have gracefully expressed in simple rhymes the sense of my privilege in having been allowed to pose as an extraordinary circumstance at the Dolores,[2] and my sympathy with its members: but it is strongly flavoured with personalities of an irreverent kind—so I don't enclose it. The old story—I am burdened with work and a distaste for a work and a necessity for working: and letters are luxuries in the writing, not to be recklessly indulged in. But you and the other ministering angels of Israel can sometimes perform an act of charity by writing to Philistia.

I wish I were going to join you in October—though I am none the less persuaded that it is better for me to be here: the practical side of me is not a strong development, but it exists and tells me that I can improve my mercenary and pecuniary prospects by imbuing myself with hateful scholarship and classical furniture generally.

Shall you come down here at all before the Long?[3]

---

1 Which pains me (daruber should be darüber). 'Junior Part' refers to a school division. The young man is unidentified.
2 The *Dolores* was a small Oxford society of seven men who met to read poetry. Founded by Ion Thynne and named for Thynne's passionate reading of Swinburne's refrain 'O bitter and tender Dolores / Our Lady of pain'.
3 The long vacation or summer holiday.

at least endeavour to persuade some one to let me personally conduct him about this Paradisal land of platitudes—it would be good for them—I don't feel entirely selfish in the suggestion.

I am casually making these remarks to you in the window of Seventh, which is a bank of flowers, arums, azaleas, κ.τ.λ: my juniors are delightfully submissive though exacting in their demands that I should do their work after the manner of such here: I am tolerably peaceful—'then the good moment goes': some repulsive drudgery of 'exact demonstration' in scholarship, or some inane 'prefects' meeting' fill up the hours: and so between reading and grinding at the mill of useless knowledge and the petty trivialities of this place, life goes—there must be another—not that it matters. Vidal[1] was intensely full of interest: analysed with his usual clear critical acumen the points of difference between you and New College—and was otherwise confidential and considerate.

I find your *Orthodox London*[2] among my possessions: enough to make you despair of getting hold of it again: I will do my possible to send it you—you know the effort is worse than a Chapel sermon.

Tell Charlie I will write: tell any one else, if that will impose upon them: my silences mean no more or less than my utterances.

You will write.

Yours in love
Lionel.

---

1 See letter 9, fn.3.
2 Charles Maurice Davis, *Orthodox London: or, Phases of Religious Life in the Church of England* (1874-5).

I have rehearsed the Commination Service,[1] inserting the Vice Chancellor[2] in each imprecation—may it do him the good I expect from it. Addio.

82
To Russell

College
[May 3, 1885]

Dearest

Many thanks for the correspondence, which I return.[3] It has amused me: my unfounded prejudices against the Master revelled in what it considered an example of his hypocritical virtues. Observe his tone: you tell him plainly that he is talking wild nonsense at random: and his answer is Fagin's again—'Have you anything to say?' 'An old man, my lord: an old man.'[4] The mild cherubicity of the sentiment! But I know nothing about the man, except that he amuses me, and thus fulfils a law of Christ. And you have at last discovered that Jessides[5] was right: 'put not your trust

---

1 A denouncing of God's anger and judgement against sinners.
2 Benjamin Jowett was Vice Chancellor of the University of Oxford, as well as being Master of Balliol College, at this time.
3 The start of the correspondence between Russell and Jowett that led to his leaving the University. See the Introduction.
4 A conflation of two scenes from Dickens' *Oliver Twist* (1838): the Artful Dodger on trial being asked, 'Have you anything to say?' and Fagin's reply to his jailer, 'An old man, my lord, a very old, old man'.
5 The son of Jesse—David.

in man,' but in yourself: for 'ye are Gods.'[1] And you compare and contrast myself with myself: and think you detect a lowered standard, a fall and decline, a decadence, a retrogression—and you think this, because this time last year I wrote about 'higher and lower' 'sin', and indulged in serenely comforting ethics generally. Well, I did all that: will repeat the process, if I consider it profitable: but verily you seem to have past [sic] out of that stage. You were in a condition of unpleasing remorse and unwholesome regret: I, knowing well enough the nature of the affliction, seriously and—may I say—with real hopes of doing something for you—set about the work of instilling comfort. And I had to select methods: to a soul or mind genuinely labouring under a burden of conscientious repentance and shame, it would had been insulting to say 'you are under a delusion: you have no burden, unless you chuse [sic] to consider that you have'—it was kinder to go through the simple process of making belief to knock it off your shoulders—'best for you and best for me'[2]—and therefore—'yes, you have sinned: but sin is an essential to salvation: the sense of sin is a sign of holiness: spirituality is recognition of sin, etc.' And what though I could not swear to my personal conviction of what I said? if it helped you at all, I surely had not done any mean or contemptible thing. I am much given to self-analysis: and often think that

---

[1] Two Psalms quoted from memory: Psalm 146:3, 'Put not your trust in Princes, nor in the son of man, in whom there is no help', and Psalm 82:6, 'I have said, Ye are gods; and all of you are children of the most High'.

[2] Meta Orred, 'In the Gloaming' (1874), composed as a popular song by Annie Fortescue Harrison in 1877.

my supreme gift of inconsistency and accommodation to varied situations is a great blessing. And don't think that my words last year were merely a curious and quaint kind of subtle pleasure to me: that I was dabbling in spiritual experiments, and had selected my nearest friend for the corpus vile: being incapable of bigotry (to put the case my way) of settled conviction (to put it yours) I cannot say now that I was insincere then: it was 'all for the best'. You think less of me? I may still pose as a friend, perhaps, but no longer as a priest of the Most High? you will write to me when you want to waste a few minutes in light and casual converse, but will keep a reproachful silence when you are spiritually inclined for sympathy? ah, that will render itself into a realistic sketch after Henry James, after Browning: but I shall not be quite so happy. And now, perhaps, your Christian nerves are being jarred and jangled into disgust? or, worst of all possibilities, you may imagine me to have assumed the very air of wounded friendship, of broken love—to be now writing under the command, at the dictation of sorrowful self-reproach. But no: I am waiting for Mass: I am perfectly calm and unmoved. And tell me what you think to be true: I may be somewhat akin to 'jesting Pilate': but I will 'stay for an answer'.[1]

Your cottage catastrophe is irritating: the idea was charming—and what will you do? I have tried to ascertain from Jack whether it will be possible for him to come down here for Concert, etc.: as yet had no answer—but I live in hope. Whithersoever I fly for refuge, cold and rain pursue after me: as though

---
1 See letter 44, fn. 5.

melancholy marked me for her own, and wanted me to write sonnets on her tender and shivering graces: just now, the rain is shrieking along a fierce wind—and the Warden[1] is to preach tonight. It is wonderfully good of Henn to write—his *métier* is charity—except when he profanes the 'Dolores' and its purposes of reading obscure versicules of unknown authors.

So you don't know when to believe me: well, is not that sense of uncertainty an element of strength to yourself? never to be sure that you have the truth from me, that you can read my meaning clear—that should be a real source of interest and a fresh motive for displaying your own transparent sincerity. It is hopeless to want to have a certainty—as Whitman will tell you—but act as though you knew, as though your action were very truth, and then you will find what you want. Human relations would be trivial enough, without this fascinating feeling of dim insight into your brothers' hearts—we may be all deceivers and deceived together. And the arrogance of certainty is a little coarse—one should be master of circumstances without the assumption of distinct knowledge about them. 'Omnis Aristippum decuit color et status et res,' quotes Pater with approval:[2] and Heraclitus with his πάντα ῥεῖ.[3] Is all this verbiage and classicalism required to prove that I am justified in laying flattering unctions to your soul, though I entertain grave

---

[1] Revd Godfrey Bolles Lee (1817-1903) was elected Warden of Winchester College in 1861. The Warden is chairman of the school's governing body.
[2] Horace, *Epistles*: All fashions, statuses, circumstances suited Aristippus.
[3] Panta rhei, all is in flux or everything flows.

doubts of their efficacy on myself—because I am well without them. I know a doctor who sent his patients to Lourdes, as tho' he believed in the miracles 'it does them good'. And these matters of spiritual, personal nature are not the daily subjects of love's study: salving souls is not the chief way of salvation. But possibly my own confession is making the situation impossible for you: very well, perhaps my confession is false—if you would prefer to think so, I will approve.

Love is larger than this: and love can include lies as well as soi disant truths: what else is the meaning of 'all in all'? Do you know Christina's 'The Convent Threshold'? it is a fragment of the Sermon on the Mount detached from the context and transfigured in the process.

Forgive all this wearisome commonplace: I only write these things because they are to me the veriest truisms of life and love. When are Mods[1] over? I wish you whatever you wish yourself. Write when you can—

Yours
Lionel

After all, where do you find this total discrepancy and disagreement? can you fasten one verbal inconsistency—in strict logic, or the lawless logic of Mill—upon me? if I said last year 'remorse is the beginning of higher things'—could I have perpetrated so banal a remark?—have I unsaid it or undone it this year? I think that my earlier scriptures were the spiritualized expressions of my life-long faith—I adopted the language of conven-

---

1 Moderation exams.

ient morality to apply it to the immoral doctrines of my personal gospel. It *is* true that 'remorse—etc': true, if you feel it: I feel that it would be true for me, if I could first feel a consciousness of sin. I said nothing that I knew to be false: for, do I know anything? I have been inconsistently consistent throughout.

83

College
[May 3, 1885]

Dearest Jack

You are making me very happy—and that is a divine faculty. But now your mention of Sark has thrown me into a passion of memories: I belong by race in part to Guernsey, and look upon the Channel Islands as my home: though without being there. But I know Sark, and how neither Hugo nor Swinburne can ever praise its absolute sublimity of loveliness—I know what it is to stand on a dark winter's night on the cliffs and watch the passion play of winds and waters and lightnings: to feel parted from life and whirled into the general life of the world: and then the gradual sinking and dying of the storm orchestra, until a sickly sun struggles over the dull coloured sea, and you know that morning is come, and that dream dead: the very thought of Sark is an enthusiasm. And you, in the laughter of the summer, can have felt the love of Sark as deeply. Ah, life has its justification, when these things are possible: and with these delights of the natural world, the kindred rapture of human love. I know that Love is God: and therefore I believe that

God is Love—the two are one and interchangeable.

Am I ever to see you with these wretched eyes of mine, before the light of the sun is taken from them? for I must become blind some day, I think. Once, I remember, you delighted me with promises to come to one of our Concerts: will you come at the end of our term here, the end of July? this place is Paradisal, and would repay you of itself the weariness of coming.

The photographer promises me myself in a week—after the manner of such. I will not forget you: in matters of this unimportance, nor in any other. Strange, to think that one year ago, and I knew neither you nor Charlie nor Osman nor Henn nor so many others—and now I cannot remember that I ever was unaware of your presence. It makes 'this unintelligible world' dear as starlight, the power of simple love upon it, the love that 'moves the sun with the other stars'.[1]

I have no time to write more, and you will at least know that it is not for lack of thoughts: though words may fail me.

Yours always
Lionel.

84

[College
May 15, 1885]

My dearest Frank

I have not written lately, because it seemed unnecessary: but now my 'insolent self-assertion' (for your

---

1 Dante's *Paradiso*, canto xxxiii, verse 145, 'L'amor che move il sole e l'altre stelle'.

ascription to me of that Whitmanlike quality, many thanks) prompts me to congratulate you, and express my real satisfaction at late occurrences.[1] You know what I hold for eternal verity: and you will know that I detest the submissive attitude. You will now be able to assert yourself—to you at least worldly considerations are no obstacle: being in the right, you will be perfectly happy. But this matter is strange enough: as an outsider, I am unable to understand the incredible fatuity of Oxford dignitaries—what do they mean by immorality? do they mean to pin definite acts upon you, or merely cast your general ideas and manner of life against you? it seems utterly unintelligible altogether. Heads of Houses would convict Jesus and John of immorality: the young man heaving upon his breast must be a stumbling block to their virtuous immaculacy.[2] For the consequences of this to others—for your people's feelings and such things—I am very downcast on your account: but what then? Jesus knew the results of the Evangel of Love, family division, discord: love necessitates that, all true action is a troubling element. Dearest, you scarcely displayed analytic acumen in your last letter: I am very self-confident and independent of others' opinions: but I cannot live without their companionship and love. Isolation is easy enough: but it is not good to be alone. And you will not suspect me of desertion and withdrawal, now: beyond all the little trivialities and mean follies

---

1 Russell has by this time been told that he will most likely be asked to leave Oxford.
2 Possible reference to Walt Whitman's lines from the *Calamus* section of *Leaves of Grass*: 'Not heaving from my ribb'd breast only, / Not in sighs at night in rage dissatisfied with myself'.

of all this matter, I recognise the high laws of freedom at stake: I can laugh at the absurdity, the gaucherie of all the case, but I am none the less determined in the truth of this matter. Believe that your life is right, that is all: it may make you, as it made me, appear arrogantly supreme in indifference to other men: but you will be right. Let me know the precise charge, if there is one: if they can point to actual facts capable of offending their vulturine nostrils, I see no other course than to accept their judgment: if they are merely vague and vindictive and venomous, face them with Walt and Jesus—defend your soul and body—either way you will be perfectly tranquil. If you go down, what does that imply? permanently or for a season? I will always do anything in my power: and I think my people will at least sympathize, though disapprove: I shall refuse, definitely, to let them or people here, restrain me in my freedom of action as to intercourse with you: unless your 'affection and respect' would prefer to cut me. As for Charlie, this will be good for his soul: it is a tangible situation, in which he must be firm one way: of course you will awhile have a certain amount of trouble and annoyance, but then that constitutes experience. And doesn't this crisis, so to say, demonstrate the truth of my position? Surely you have acted according to your will or conscience: and this is the result. Oh, I am not inhuman, but rather all human: with all my nature developed. But I have a control over all passion which you lack: I can appear unreal and cold and insincere and contemptuous and contemptible, whilst you are simply natural. I had a letter from a cousin lately in which she says 'You live artificially naturally: I live in chaos'. That was true: my life is a study. And now you are in a position of crucial importance: don't be carried away, and don't be obstinate: be simply indifferent: show that you can not and will not dishonour yourself by accepting their dicta and dogmata: laugh, be interested happily, being conscious of the eternal truth as it is in Whitman. The world is very old and vast: the Vice-Chancellor is not a Phidian Zeus, that he may control the world. Ridding, Spooner, these people will not really abandon you: they will not admire you: nor will they dislike you: all things are good.

So far as I could see, until this business came about, I should have been most happy to stay a few days with Charlie and yourself—but of course this may alter things for you. Don't think I am in any way anxious to stand well before any faction of this world: scandal has no terror and much amusement for me. Still the infinite triviality of the affair confuses me: how can the Warden of Merton[1] and Spooner, etc, actively concern themselves in the matter of your morality? I am so used to living my own life undisturbed and unquestioned that it seems monstrous that you should be worried with the impertinent interference of limited Christians. Shelley with atheism or deism, Landor with rowdiness, I can understand:[2] but not

---

1 George Charles Brodrick (1831-1903) was the don whom it was later revealed found the 'immoral letter' Russell had supposedly written. Much later Russell described him as 'always a very good friend to me'.

2 Shelley was sent down from University College, Oxford in 1811 after writing and disseminating a pamphlet entitled 'The Necessity of Atheism'. Walter Savage Landor (1775-1864), poet

how you can conflate the two with personal conduct of life—that is surely, unless it actively becomes a social nuisance, your own matter. As to Marson, in ignorance of the facts I cannot speak: it has an air of unholy conventionalism[1]—perhaps I have no right to say so. How do people take your case? I mean the Dolores set? I imagine they know of it. What Oxford at large would be likely to say, is easily imagined. You would not feel scruples as to coming here? Surely not, when people here would not be likely to come in your way aggressively. Has my name turned up again? apparently there is no accounting for any possible turn and twist in the evolution of scandal—at least, as far as you are concerned, I can thoroughly defend both of us—beyond that there would be no need to go. But I am entirely sick of this prolonged state of armed suspicion: we must, all of us, live such lives as we know the best for us—and regulate our conduct so as to avoid active offence of an unreasonable kind to others: further than that we need not be careful to justify our ways. This leads, no doubt, to arrogance: it introduces innumerable doubts and heart breakings: makes you distrust me, me condescend to every one, Christians dislike both of us: well, all that seems inevitable. Here you have definite ground: are you or not to be your own judge and standard? I know that the advice is bad from the worldly aspect: but, plainly, I would declare to my people that my

---

and author, was sent down from Trinity College in 1794 for firing a gun at the window of a fellow student whose late-night revelries disturbed him.
1 See letter 35, fn.1.

life was rapidly becoming impossible, without more freedom: leave Oxford as soon as you can, leave every thing: go somewhere, and do what you will. Absurdly out of the question for one in your position of life, I suppose: damn positions in life and all things as by Christian and respectable sociology established. Then, too, I don't know what either you or Charlie mean to do in life: and this business may have serious results in that direction. But still the main course is clear: 'dismiss whatever insults your own soul'.[1] Perhaps you will look askance at advice or sympathy coming from my heartless heights of Epicureanism: that I can't help. Let me really know whether I can do or write any thing that may help you in any way: I don't know the facts of the case, but if any thing lies in my power, I will not hesitate to do it: I don't precisely see how I could actively help you. On the whole, this hardly seems a situation calling for much pity: such pity as I do feel, mainly has my elders and betters, my pastors and masters, for its objects. Who are actually the prime movers in this matter? and whence do they obtain their knowledge? There is beautiful spring weather here: I am peacefully writing English verse, and feeling kind toward the Race: and this fiasco is a false note: makes me smile, likewise shudder: it is so grotesque. You are not over disturbed I imagine. Yet I am sorry: that simple and infantine expression just is the right one here: sorry for the harassing folly of it all, the mere ugliness of its inanity: the world of beasts and flowers and waters is so perfect, the world of men

---

1 From Walt Whitman's 'Preface' to the 1855 edition of *Leaves of Grass*.

and women and emasculate Christians is so fatuous. Read Whitman: he will never fail you, that is the test of divinity: Jesus and Shelley and Whitman, they are steadfast in faith, never wavering. Men think—men like Ridding even—that the Whitman doctrine is a mean, unwholesome poison trying to pass for the breath of God: they talk of 'moral sanitation': that love must be eschewed, when it claims domination and lordship upon the flesh: that life is to be a solemn and dignified affection and kindly good naturedness. We believe and know that life is something more than that: we justify the existence of evil by denying its existence. 'Behold the Lamb of God, that taketh away the sins of the world!' has that a meaning? verily I find a plain meaning in it: I believe it to be an exact and scientific statement of an unending and essential truth. Ah Frank, here you are facing the hatefullest enemy of the light: the Christian virtue that is keen scented after vice, sharp eyed after offences. Well, if our faith is anything more than a puerile waste of plausible words, now you have the occasion to prove it: it is easy to confront the indifferent and the sinners: it is the active moralists whom we must be able to confront: it is the men such as Ridding, full of love and faith and enthusiasm, whom we must not collapse before: either we are humbugs and shams, or we are convicted enthusiasts: either we mean something, or we only say it. I am not trying to excite you to headstrong rebellion: I merely wish to assert the reality of our faith: that is, if we do hold it. You have lately reproached me with my self-assertion, assumption of omniscience, and spoken of your own conscience, your ideas of right and wrong: there would seem to be a difference somewhere. Well, if your 'conscience' accuses you, don't be hypocritical, don't swear you are innocent: *mea maxima culpa* is your fitting formula. But if, as I believe, we are really at one, then let them see that the faith of an infinite love, infinite tolerance, infinite pride, infinite compassion,—that this faith is indeed from everlasting and world without end. If you are in earnest: that is all. You may think it best to come to terms: well, that may be best, I don't know the facts: at least the faith must be left holy and undefiled. Jesus is ascended, the faith reigns—away from all clashing dogma and creed, away from the strife of tongues, there, in the clear beauty of the spring skies, there is Jesus the divine Love: not Jowett, mumbling senile scraps of Plato-cum-Prayer Book, but Christ Jesus, very God, very Man, the power of God and the Word of God, the Lamb of God that taketh away the sins of the World. Believe it as you will—poetical fancy, dream, vision, fable, myth, lie—still there throbs through its infinite wonder the truth of its infinite Love. We are jealous and cold and distrustful: I coldly analyse, you passionately abuse: fools both, whilst the faith is one and indivisible.

Write to me how things pass: how the world demeans itself—it is intensely fascinating to watch the tortuous virtues uncoiling their speckled lack-lustre folds: all mental or spiritual calisthenics are attractive. At least, if circumstances compel you to leave Oxford and break off your present life, none of your friends worth the name will consider you unclean, a moral leper to taboo and drive into the deserts of repentance—and then all this ineffable folly will be at an end—you will be your own master legally very soon—spiritually, really, we are always our own masters.

I trust nothing I have said has offended you: though it does wear an aspect of appreciative sympathy, you will believe that it is true enough? I never mean to be unkind to any one—pas même[1] the evangelicals.

Jowett must have behaved shamefully—can he imagine that he is furthering his pet scheme of seeing you 'a useful and distinguished' respectability, by disgusting you with his own example of those qualities of utility and distinction?

Feel assured that I will not renounce you—I must reiterate that.

For the present, I must stop here—

always yours
Lionel.

'Is victory great? do we think victory great?
So it is,—But now it seems to me,
When it cannot be helped, that defeat is great,
And that death and dismay are great.'[2]

85

College
[May 21, 1885]

My dearest Frank

Love prevails always: it prevails inevitably—the

---

1 Not even.
2 Johnson quotes from memory the last verse of Whitman's 'To a Foil'd European Revolutionaire' (1856).

lordship of love through sorrow and suffering and trial—prevails to the end. Triumph is assured, through failure, through defeat: I congratulate you. For the correspondence,—that is variously beautiful—Brodrick's the most touching: he appears so honestly loving. Ridding is cruelly sincere—he thinks that—but is wrong enough: Aristotle is not flesh and soul and spirit—only mind working on experience—which is Gehenna, our minds being finite and infinitesimal. Blind, blind—Henn, the Warden, blind, all blind—yet the sun shines, and there is light. If some of the priests who counsel submission, knew the meaning of such peace! had Zimri peace?[1] would you have peace, having slain your master Love, done him despite, crucified the Lord afresh? ah, it is no cause of sorrow, no cause of despair—it is bitter, the division of kindred: but the division of brotherhood were bitter unto death. Your Christian accuser may well be left to himself and his standard of honourable dealing—God forgive him, and the devil take him. For my words you express thanks: well, they are merely I, merely my life: I know, in my arrogance of certitude, I know the truth: the truth that will make whole. You wrong me: but I acknowledge that you are right, being you, to reject the Church. I still cling to her universal possibilities—not for ease, not from fear, but from faith and love. No true efforts clash—the world is all subject to love in any form. That we may leave awhile—practically, ordination has become impossible for you. We are at one in heart. You say that your grandmother knows no facts: does she know enough to justify me

---

1 2 Kings 9:31, 'And as Jehu entered in at the gate, she said, Has Zimri peace, who slew his master?'

in a simple letter expressing my faith in you and your honour? if it were not intrusive, with your approval I would write: not as a preacher of Whitman, but as a Christian gentleman, known to her as your friend. I lunch with the Daker on Sunday—one question—can you answer me by then? understand me: have you technically incurred legal penalties? don't be angry: you don't suspect me. Mrs Dick is injudicious, and publicly alluded to the matter: not in a marked way, and I have taken precautions: me of course you may rely upon.

I must leave off this. I shall remember you at the Eucharist on Sunday—

I will write to Charlie—he will not resent that.
Always yours in all faith and love.
Lionel.

86
To Russell

College
[May 30, 1885]

Dearest

I both should and would have written, but affairs here have kept me occupied—the old story, schoolboy immorality resulting in expulsion, i.e., wreck of definite prospects: the victim now is Taylor, my colleague in my chamber:[1] a man I am very fond of, and a thoroughly good man in the sight of God, and a lover of Shelley—but morality demands his suppres-

---

1 Arnold Charles Taylor (1867-unknown) was expelled for 'immoral behaviour'.

sion, and he has departed home to his mother, a poor widow, and a crippled brother—that is the way of the world—that is virtue and the Kingdom of Christ. On Monday next I shall not have much leisure time—but between two and four I should be able to scrape together spare hours,—yes, I could see you again then, if you can think it worth your while. Charlie answered a letter of mine most nobly and firmly—and wants me to stay with him some days in August, and see Jack—and I have accepted with joy. The Daker was absolutely thunderstruck at the possibility of the charge—'whether true or not, it's the last thing I should associate with him' but he seems to think an honourable compromise possible—but he does not really understand the case fully: his sympathies are of course with you. The world, Ridding, the Daker,—all the good men are against us.

Hugo's death is magnificent, full of the glory of his supreme life—I would give anything to be able to see his face and kiss his lips. There is no man living who is worthy to stand beside him, but Whitman—and he will pass to the dark soon. A pilgrimage to him is one of my fixed purposes some day.

Osman has written at length, and seems disposed to take our side. But the world is so strange—Hugo is dead, my friend here exiled—and the saints jubilant everywhere.

I shall be very pressed with work for the few ensuing weeks, and letters will be things merely of necessity—but at all times I will be happy in doing anything you ask of me.

Always yours
Lionel

87
To Sayle

[College
May 31, 1885]

Dearest

Your letter reaches me amid a fortunate coincidence of Osman, Jack, and some others—I am fulfilled with a multitude of cursing and blessing from you all. This is at least a 'laugh provoking' catastrophe—perhaps it has more weighty elements. Life is pleasant everywhere and everyhow. Yes, if you are able to endure it, I am perfectly free to inflict myself upon you—almost at any date between August 1st and Sept 1st, and inasmuch as Winchester might be less paradisal than usual for you, that seems the only alternative delight. But in my selfish voracity I don't see why Jack should not also come to our Concert—you see it is better that he should meet the full summer glory of Winchester than that he should meet me—the place is at least of equal value—yes, I must adhere to that—if Jack will not be alarmed at the prospect. With all possible indulgence for scandal and prurient exercise of imagination, I still think it somewhat unreasonable of the Christians to delight their virtuous souls with repulsive speculations—what possible pleasure lies for them in the matter? Already casual men I know have written conciliating little appeals to me to tell them what is of truth about Russell, as one who knows the facts, and I am weary with ejaculating 'guardians'.

Frank is rather vague: seems to have no precise ideas of his future line of action—perhaps inevitably so. 'Preaching the truth' has an air of the grotesque—what is not truth? accept every thing, surely, even Christian virtue: there is no sorrow, no evil—unless you make them.

I have had no satisfactory exposition of the worldly view of the case. Henn sagely remarks that he does not take my position: Jack confesses that he accepts the triumphant aspect now, but did not before. What possible reason have our friends 'of the virtue'? 'What say they?'

If Whitman would become the general creed, England would surpass old Athens, modern Paris, modern New York. Whitman has the vitality, the virtue of Philistia, transmuted to a deathless and crystal strength of spirit—war and art would be perfected in him. But Whitman is á dream, except for the few who know him—has his night visions, too, of Christian virtues and Vice-Chancellors—and the awakening is brusque, deficient in refinement. One disastrous outcome of this is Frank's absolute refusal to accept the priesthood—now, when such as he are demanded for the priesthood—his strong 'sense of duty'—curses on that abstraction when it takes shape—will not suffer him do violence to his reason and his conviction—what a depth of wrongheadedness appears to me there! well, he would never be quite happy in the pale of my beautiful city of music and lights and flowers and incense and Leaves of Grass—that is a visioned Hesperid island, never to be realized. You saw Ridding's answer to Frank? not a spark of affection—quietly satirical and practical and scarifying—likewise entirely foolish, with a wise folly all Ridding's own—a part of his unique charm. Aristotle omnipresent with a dash of common sense—versus Whitman and super-sensuous truths. As to Apuleius, a person of great attraction to me,—he was from 120 or thereabouts—which is the date, roughly, of Marcus Aurelius and Lucian—but it is of little importance, so long as one can read the man. I was with the Daker last Sunday—by Frank's advice, I gave him the outlines of the story, under the necessary fudge of secrecy in general: he could not, any more than can I, comprehend the fatuous folly of the authorities—provided that you were really, as he puts it, innocent—which is a large word, and intended by Whitman to include the world, even the Christians. I am spreading Whitman here—and lead him largely to those who can bear him—tho' the authorities do refuse him for the Library. Is Richards[1] an orthodox Christian? I have encountered here an old Wykehamist, by name Dering,[2] who is engaged in promoting a pestilence of Bible reading in public schools, who tells me he has captured Richards—which is distressing, if true. This is not really very lamentable: it will at least bring some people to recognize the existence of the free love evangel—as a sacred thing, not a 'meanly corruption of pure virtues' to quote from Ridding a term he once applied to a statement of mine in self defence.

---
1 See letter 73, fn 2.
2 Two men named Dering went to Winchester: George Edwardes (1841-1902) and Lionel Ashton (1850-90), both became barristers.

I wish you well through Mods—if not, what matters it or anything? trite, but true. I hope to see Osman and Percy[1] here after Mods—when I may hear their views and ideas on the matter.

Don't inconvenience your arrangements—but could you give me even a general idea of a possible date at which I could be with you, if that is to be? other matters rather hang on that for me.

Work is somewhat pressing now—so am unable to write at length. 'Finally, my brother be strong.'[2]

always yours
Lionel

88

College
[June 7, 1885]

Dearest Jack

Of course you will come to Winchester—as though it was for the sake of seeing me that you were to come! Frank will be here—likewise, I hope, Harry,[3] with whom I have yet to become acquainted—you must be with us. You could come on Saturday 25th, so as to have a Sunday here, the Concert is the next night, and the peculiar institution known to us as 'Domum' on Tuesday: we go down on Wednesday. As to Charley's kind proposal, the first part of August would suit me best—and the earlier, the better for some other arrange-

---

1 Johnson refers to Henn here and later by his Christian name.
2 Ephesians 6:10.
3 Henry Currie Marillier (1865-1951), then at Cambridge, later Managing Director of William Morris & Co.

ments of mine. So that if it would suit him, I should be perfectly free to go to him from Winchester, at once—but no time would be absolutely impossible for me. You will come? I fear I know of no one who would be able to give you hospitality, since the place is infested with old Wykehamists—but I can easily secure you a room somewhere. Percy and Osman intend to come down on Tuesday—which will be delightful, also amusing. Frank, who naturally was unable to pass through Winchester without staying a few hours, seemed singularly happy—but for the plague of relatives. But all the fortunes and friendships of our little lives seem swallowed up in the thought of Hugo's death—it is as though the sun were stricken blind in heaven, and the voice of the sea were silent for ever—one does not look for the death of the sun and sea, for all their centuries—and yet Hugo, the elemental spirit of the world's poetry, is dead. The impression of it is physical, actual. And the majesty of the French people in their sorrow! well, Whitman liveth—and he is light of light. Yes, Richards foolishly inserted a rhapsody of mine—with a casual misprint here and there which increased the poetry of the original[1]—poor Rugby, with its taste gradually educated up to that! Do you know Welldon, the new head of Harrow?[2] he preached here the other day the most perfectly beautiful sermon that I can remember: the man's face is very winning. He told me that he would rather be going anywhere than to Harrow—which he detests.

A Christian wants me to talk to him—*hélas*.

always yours
Lionel J

---

1 'In Dreams' was published in *The Leaflet*, May 1885.
2 James Edward Cowell Welldon (1854-1937).

89

College
[June 1885][1]

My dearest Charlie

Merely a word—of salutation and answer. Since you do really expect me in your kindness, I declare myself ready indeed to come to you.

Our term ends on the 28th July—i.e., leave here on the 29th. Would it suit you to receive me that day?

I expect Jack: heard from him, to my delight, this morning. He has a photo of me which is not unlike—but rather petulant and scornful—anything but my humble toleration.

I have not thanked you for the Song—I do thank you. Don't look for letters—I am not up to them.

always yours
Lionel J

90
To Russell

College
[July 14, 1885]

Dearest

Just a word, a greeting—no time for more. Salute

---

[1] Incorrectly sequenced and dated March 1885 by Russell. More correctly dated by reference to recent communication from Badley and his proposed visit.

Harry from me—we must meet at Domum. Even far away in Wales, my dear mother has heard rumours of you—so far as I can gather, from other relatives in town—but the Second Master wrote her a magnificent defence of you, and I have assured her perturbed spirit with assertions of your true and Catholic situation—without going into details. I think my people will give no more trouble. Jack, whom I have imagined free from such annoyance, is uncertain whether he will be able to come to you—but he will do his possible to overcome opposition. He is at Cambridge now, after dreaming lazily by the northern sea. I was at the Daker's yesterday—he hopes to be able to visit you, but is not certain—poor Malise alters things.[1] Who will come to Winchester? and whom will Mrs Dick receive?—because if Jack is coming, I must get him a room somewhere fairly soon—the place will be crowded to death. My dear uncle will be down, with, I hope and trust, my copyiste [*sic*] cousin—whom we must make you known to—unless his sober senses have been perverted by rumour, likely to startle him into a care for proprieties.

As to the English verse, I am satisfied—I had a vow to make them accept blank verse—I intend to make an Elizabethan quasi-epic—all the beautiful heroes who lived lives worth living, and knew they were men with passions—and got on in the world at the same time. Congratulations on the tutor—stealing a march on the guardians—a perfect Sophoclean irony in the

---

1 Malise Cunninghame Graham (1860-85), curate of St John's, on whose early death Johnson wrote a series of lyrics ('In Memory', *Poems* [1895]).

idea of perverting his pure and pastoral mind. They are—i.e., W. M. Rossetti and the Gilchrists, etc.—getting up a subscription in support of Whitman, who is destitute of means and unable to work—curious to see how the appeal will be answered. Imagine—a heat visible and tangible and audible, burning away to the heart of the world—a sky of liquid fiery sapphire—and withal, three weeks' detestable exams—it will kill me. In fact, I refuse to work at all: I read Lucretius in the sunshine—or Hugo. Class lists are satisfactory—I don't imagine Charlie expected anything higher. With love to every one,

Yours in love
Lionel

91

College
[July 19, 1885]

Dearest Jack

I cannot go to Charlie's—but if you still care to come, come, and I will do what I can to repay you. Neither can I go to Russell's. I have no time for further explanations. At least this is no fainteartedness or desertion of mine: you will believe that?

always yours
Lionel.

We shall never meet—but I could not love you better than I do, dear brother.

92

College
[July 21, 1885]

Dearest Frank

I am so sorry for this last unhappiness—it is for you such exile, such loss of Paradise.[1] And apart from the loss of Winchester, it is another friendship lost in the flesh awhile—and, even though I am cold and inhuman, I think you will be a little grieved even for that. Yes, so far as personal intercourse goes, I can see no other course than submission, not in spirit, but to inevitable compulsion—and here I am an unit of many units, and the recognition of the devil by one is his recognition by all—which may not be allowed. But I will strenuously stand out for correspondence—on social, common sense, Christian grounds—on that point I will refuse my father submission—for that is my personal affair, not compromising him as the head of a family, or the school of which I am a member. But I have heard nothing as yet from him. Dick has written to him—but he is not in England—and I shall know soon.

Dick is very kind—talked much to me—asserts his faith in your innocence of motives, if not in your acts—but considers himself bound in honour, as a public servant, not to take personal feelings into account. Mrs Dick is terribly sad—I never believed her capable of very deep emotion—she seems heart-

---
1 Russell was asked to stay away from Winchester as news of his expulsion from Oxford spread.

broken. Your answer to Dick puzzles them—they don't understand it at all. Oh, this estrangement of spirits, this miserable sundering of idea—I want to break away—but am fettered here altogether. I have heard nothing as to Charlie, but have written to break off the visit, thinking that best. At the risk of seeming obtrusive, let me ask you whether you still think him worthy of your sacrifice? I will send a photo—I have none by me, but have ordered some—but I think better of my mother than to suppose she will be unwilling to regard you as a human being, even a friend. If only people would see things clearly, would try to understand! but some curse is on them with blindness. I don't know whether Jack is coming, now that I do not go with him to Cambridge—I almost hope he will not.[1] Ah, he is unspeakably loving—I would rather not see him. Don't be troubled, if you do not hear from me just yet—after Thursday I am fairly free. Mrs Dick will be with you tomorrow:[2] she will give you my love and try, better than I can, to tell you all I feel or think. Speak out, they all cry: guilty or not guilty? clear yourself, etc—what can you do? is it so new a thing to us, this triumph of truth and love through reproach and evil speaking all bitterness of death? 'I go in for expediency'—no, but I do not defy ἀνάγκη[3] even in the shape of a father and a schoolmaster—that is impossible—when master of

---

1 He did not: the two men only met once in the flesh, when Johnson was at Oxford.
2 By this time Russell had taken a house in Hampton-on-Thames. Mrs Richardson was the only one of his elders to visit him there.
3 Anagkē, fate or necessity.

myself, my action is my own—not now, by facts and law—in spirit and speech, I own no control. Jowett is very foolish—Fearon has told me that he has heard wild stories of me and Jowett's displeasure with me—I don't see through it at all.

I cannot write more now—I shall not see you, but—

'Oh! je suis avec vous! j'ai cette sombre joie;
Ceux qu'on accable, ceux qu'on frappe,
   et qu'on foudroie
M'attirent: je me sens leur frére.'[1]

Ah, though even the good saints are blind in their kindness, yet

'il faut bien quelqu'un qui soit pour les étoiles!'[2]

I began melancholy: now I am laughing—there is summer and the thought of love, Sappho of Lesbos, and the soft winds—and the vice-chancellor with the authorities. It is real, but very insignificant. They bar you from Winchester—that is miserable—but then that is not all. I believe in the Communion of Saints, the forgiveness of sins, the assertion of the body, and the love everlasting.

Give Harry my love—

always in love
Lionel.

Don't show this to Mrs Dick—she is so kind—and she would be distressed.

---

1 Opening lines from Victor Hugo's *L'Année terrible* (1872), 'Juin'. In literal translation: 'Oh! I am with you! I feel this dark joy; / Those they oppress, those they beat and strike down / Attract me: I feel I am their brother'.
2 Hugo's *L'Année terrible*, 'Juillet: La Voix Haut': 'someone must be for the stars!'

93

[August 5, 1885]

Dearest Frank

I too have not written—for Harry ~~is~~ was with you, which is enough. My father is impenetrable: professes real affection for you, but resolutely declines to sanction correspondence—on pains of rejection and expulsion and disinheriting, etc—whilst he has told the Winchester people to stop letters passing. So that the mere power of choice is gone—there is nothing for me to do. I have pointed out that his action has no reason in it—that my sympathies, etc, are only strengthened by silence—he does not see it. So, until I am legally master of myself, I must say goodbye—they know not what they do.

Yours and my own only
Lionel.

It is only now that I fully realise the force of Shelley's invectives against 'custom'—how it enslaves and encircles and paralyzes—the Dicks full of love, tied by their official position—and so with all of us—none of us free agents, oppressors or oppressed: all under the domination of Frankenstein—it makes one laugh more than most other jests. And in ten years—how miserable this will seem. I am definitely cut off by facts from you and Sayle—Harry is looked upon askance—the general social communion of several others broken up—distrust and distress introduced—

and for a nothing—because custom is violated and her virgin shame exposed as worthless. I can't write—I have no will to leave you with words of anything but peace—but damn the world at least.

What are the rumours? and from whom do you hear of them? I have impressed upon Mrs Dick the necessity of silence from even mention of you in public here.

In haste. I can't imagine what rumours can have spread, unless Percy mistook some remarks of mine. Edgar[1] was in Hall lately, and suddenly turned to me and said, 'Is it true that Russell has been sent down for immorality or atheism or something?' with a few similar remarks. I, as shortly as possible, satisfied him with a negation. The conversation was public—but quite momentary. That is absolutely the only occasion on which I have mentioned your name at Winchester to any one any where, except the Daker. Any rumours that may be circulating—I have heard none—must necessarily come from other sources. I have reason to believe that more people at Oxford know generally the truth of the case, than you think—of course, without facts or names—merely that morality is mixed up in it.

Yrs
L.

---

1 Most likely Wilfred Haythorne Edgar (1864-1936), later a barrister.

APPENDIX

The original publication *Some Winchester Letters of Lionel Johnson* opened with the following Browning verses and introduction and closed with a poem by Johnson.

Not on the vulgar mass
Called "Work," must sentence pass,
Things done, that took the eye and had the price;
O'er which, from level stand,
The low world laid its hand,
Found straightway to its mind, could value in a trice:

But all the world's coarse thumb
And finger failed to plumb,
So passed in making up the main account:
All instincts immature,
All purposes unsure,
That weighed not as his work, yet swelled the man's account:

Thoughts hardly to be packed
Into a narrow act,

Fancies that broke through language and escaped:
All I could never be,
All men ignored in me,
This, I was worth to God, whose wheel the pitcher shaped.

> RABBI BEN
> EZRA

INTRODUCTION

It is thought that these letters, written by a scholar of the College of St. Mary, Winton, may be of interest to a wider circle than that to which they were originally addressed, in several respects. In the first place it will be observed that they deal not with personal or temporary affairs, but with general questions of a kind which have interested the whole thinking part of the whole human race for centuries. They are further remarkable as the production of a schoolboy between the ages of sixteen and eighteen; showing as they do a most unusually extensive acquaintance with English literature and a great sense of values. It is true on looking back from the vantage-ground of middle age one may detect traces of immaturity, such as the excessive praise of Emerson, but these are few and far between. The letters also appear to have an interest, at any rate to contemporaries, in bringing again before one's mind's eye some of the outstanding figures of the late Victorian age. So it has been thought that though the class to which such a collection would appeal may be small, none the less to them its appeal would be a real one.

My first recollection of Lionel Johnson is as a small College man with that pale oval face of the frontispiece to *Poetical Works* reproduced from the very photograph referred to in these letters. It was set off by the severe College gown, and suggested even to a Philistine something wistful and appealing. My own acquaintance with him really began in the school library, where he assisted me with suggestions as to the books I should read. It remained throughout rather on the literary and philosophic plane than on any basis of great personal intimacy. Though a year or two my junior, and though I had for him a passionate devotion and admiration which still survives after thirty-five years, my prevailing attitude to him was one of reverence and awe. As he says more than once in his letters, he appeared to be unimpressionable, unemotional, undemonstrative—in a word, he walked through life aloof like some ascetic saint. My own temperament was the exact converse, and I recognize that I was often chilled by this aloofness, although I believe, so far as his nature permitted it, he was fond of me and valued my friendship.

Oxford saw the beginning of the tragedy which culminated in his early cutting off and the loss to the world of another genius. The poor boy! the wonderful child! the loving angel! for an angel of God he was undoubtedly intended to be, and in all associations in my memory of him was and still is. I care nothing for such external facts about his life as have been forced upon my notice, I care nothing for the measure of the world's coarse thumb, this, and no less, was he worth to God, whose wheel the pitcher shaped.

Filled always with a passionate desire to protect and to cherish, I was hopelessly and inevitably thwarted by the very facts of the situation. He had, as he explains in one of his own letters, an arid home life, a lonely school life. What he wanted was a mother and a wife, or a wife who would have been a mother, as all good wives are: some simple loving human thing to cherish him against the cold and alien world and to enable his spirit to move undimned [*sic*] along its natural path. Look at these extracts from his letters, and compare them pityingly with the pitiable truth: "I have one monotone to which I will intone my life: I will be a priest."... "I long... to live in seclusion... infusing beauty and the simplicity of love... into minds fresh from God and the great sea. And after that... to wear out the best of my life in our great towns. What an ambition! Sincerely, what an almost inconceivable aim: and oh, to realize it!"... "I go about my daily trivialities with the words of the Most High on my closed lips and in my heart, breaking for a little love."... "But to one who, like myself, believes that he has the truth in inspiration, personal, uncommunicable truth, it is very hard to be able to use it, to feel himself a temple of the Holy Ghost, yet see in himself no signs of sacrifice."... "I think I shall not die yet— that I shall waste on into old age and memories of a beautiful life: for life is meaningless without beauty, and everything is, or becomes at need, beautiful." Yet these extracts show the true Lionel: not only the later genius of "The Art of Thomas Hardy," but the loving, suffering man, burning with zeal to help and comfort his fellow-sufferers in the world. I have him to thank for the love of Browning, for an outlook on life which has been my salvation in many a dark hour, and for a contribution of courage and high hope. Would that he might have lived to the full the life for which he was intended, and that his message and his influence might have been known to a wider circle! But it was not to be.

THE EDITOR.

March 1919.

Under the moon's high glory, and all stars
Fluting their night-song, brother of my love.
As by their light I take upon their lips
Thy heart's gold-starry song, love-laden winds
Linger within the music, and the night
Murmurs. Love, Love,—how all the world
Leaps to the lyre of love, and clear, far spheres
Clash out to love their music: and all seas
Sway to the thrill of love! and now this night
That floats into the pulsing land of dreams
Where memories are soft, thy love hath turned
To preludes, that before the terrible sun
Strike his great note of thunder, I may drink
Low laughter from thy lips, and bear mine own
To thy fair well of sorrow, and may wash
My feet within thy tears. Now our Lord Love
Give thee to fling his music on all airs
That earth-dimmed eyes may take pure peace, to feel
Love's whisper cool upon their throb, and lips

Dust-littered from the earth may lilt awhile
Love's melodies, inspired to know the stars
Wherefrom Love looks in blessing, and to catch
Love's musical soul in all dream silences.
And clang of dreadful hatred. Brother
Brother within the cloudland canst thou see
Thrones set in the larger air stream, whence all life
Shall pour high ecstasies and utter Love
That spheres must shout to hearken as they whirl
Down the full seas of space? shall we end so?
Yes, we shall not one die, for music lives.
And life is Love's best music. Life and Love.
And Music—an these be, can men and women
Die from upon the earth? we shall not die:
But live, by love and music.

INDEX OF PEOPLE, PLACES, AND INSTITUTIONS (EXCLUDING CORRESPONDENTS)

Aeschylus, 87, 89
Apuleius, 263
Aristotle, 258, 263
Arnold, Edwin, 61, 65, 70
Arnold, Matthew, 56, 63, 65, 91, 151, 153, 177, 208, 226
Bacon, Francis, 180, 245
Balliol College, Oxford, 21, 36, 55, 72, 74, 92, 171, 223, 231, 236, 242, 243
Baudelaire, Charles, 157
Bedales School, 44
Beddoes, Thomas Lovell, 106-107, 121, 214
Bennet, Ernest William, 203
Benson, Godfrey Rathbone, 84
Billson, Charles James, 113
Blake, William, 124, 135-136, 224, 226, 228, 235, 238
Blavatsky, Helena ('Madam'), 61-62, 87, 174
Booth, William, 84
Burdon-Sanderson, John, 88

Buxton Forman, Henry, 224
Bradlaugh, Charles, 59, 91, 155, 162
Broderick, George Charles, 40, 252, 258
Brontë, Emily, 118, 156
Broughton, Rhoda, 228
Browning, Robert, 29, 44, 56, 57, 58-61, 64, 70, 96, 97, 100, 105-107, 116-118, 123, 136, 137, 139, 140, 145, 151, 154, 155, 156, 164, 171, 188-189, 190, 197, 202, 204, 207, 238, 245, 274-275
Browning, Elizabeth Barrett, 111, 140, 151, 156, 174, 213
Buchanan, Robert, 208
Byron, George Gordon, sixth Baron Byron, 103, 123
Cambridge, University of, 7, 11, 16, 27, 44, 47, 49, 51, 115, 201, 202, 216, 267, 270
Capel, Thomas John, 174
Carlyle, Thomas, 99, 103, 203
Castle Howard, Yorkshire, 179
Catullus, 162, 235, 238
Chatterton, Thomas, 149
Chaucer, Geoffrey, 162
Chillingworth, William, 162
Chopin, Frédéric, 205-206, 235, 238l.
Church of England, 31, 56-57, 60, 63, 127-128, 131-132, 133-134, 139, 142, 143, 146, 147, 154, 157-158, 160-162, 166, 172-176, 178-187, 201
Clifford, William Kingdon, 91-92
Clough, Arthur Hugh, 207, 208, 214-215
Coles, Edward and Alfred, 203
Collins, Wilkie, 171
Comte, Auguste, 71, 100-101, 104, 143, 144, 146, 171, 175

Cumberland, Stuart, 153
Cunninghame Graham, Malise, 267
Curran, Amelia, 224
Crawford, F. Marion, 62
Cruickshank, Alfred Hamilton, 113, 150
Dante, 139, 148, 155, 249
Darwin, Charles, 140
David, Rhys, 77
Davis, Charles Maurice, 242
Democratic Federation, The, 75
Dickins, Charles, 111, 243
Dickins, Henry Compton ('the Daker'), 74, 76, 84, 166, 222, 225-226, 259, 260, 263, 267, 273
Dolores, The, 33, 240, 246, 253
Douglas, Lord Alfred Bruce, 8
Dowson, Ernest, 8
Dublin, 12
Du Boulay, J. T. H., 88-89
Earle, Adrian, 15
Edgar, Wilfred Haythorne, 273
Edwards, Herbert Edward Osman, 231-232, 235, 249, 260, 261, 264, 265
Ellicott, Charles, 178
Eliot, George, 101, 104, 109, 121
Eliot, T.S., 14
Emerson, Ralph Waldo, 112, 144, 146, 153, 157, 176, 178
Farrar, Dean Frederick William, 225
Faulkner, Charles Joseph, 224
Fearon, William Andrewes, 131, 167, 198, 221, 271
Ferishtah, Hampton-on-Thames, 44, 270
Ferrier, David, 171

Fichte, Johann Gottlieb, 144, 146
Field, Michael, 12
Fillingham, Robert Charles, 224, 236
Fisher, Herbert, 88
Fitzroy Street, London, 11, 12
Fletcher, Ian, 34
Fort, James Alfred, 83
Fox-Pitt, St George Lane, 21, 70
Fraser, James, 139, 174
Gilchrist, Anne, 268
Gladstone, William, 28, 84
Goethe, Johann Wolfgang von, 105, 119, 170, 176, 178, 240
Gordon, Charles George, 152, 166, 171
Green, Sidney Faithorn, 174
Grotius, 170
Guernsey, Channel Islands, 248
Guizot, François, 138
Hardy, Henry John, 87, 113
Hardy, Thomas, 12
Harrison, Annie Fortescue, 244
Harrison, Frederic, 102, 110, 114, 153, 158, 190
Harrow School, 265
Hartmann, Eduard von, 146, 226
Haweis, Hugh Reginald, 150
Hawkins, Charles, 79
Heine, Heinrich, 155, 159, 162, 237
Henn, Percy Umfreville, 34, 244, 228, 231-232, 236, 240, 246, 249, 258, 262, 264, 265
Heraclitus, 246
Hood, Thomas, 140
Hooker, Richard, 162

Horace, 246
Horne, Herbert, 11
Horton, Robert Forman, 122
Howard, George James, ninth earl of Carlisle, 179
Howard, Rosalind Frances, countess of Carlisle, 179
Howells, William Dean, 109
Hugo, Victor, 106, 131, 172, 178, 209, 238, 248, 260, 265, 268, 271
Image, Selwyn, 11
Ingersoll, Robert G., 155
Jacobi, Carl Gustav Jacob, 144
James, Henry, 245
Jepson, Edgar, 231, 236
John, the Apostle, 88, 91, 237, 250
Johnson, William Victor, 23, 25-26, 31, 43, 93-94, 100, 108-109, 110-111, 163, 221, 269, 272
Johnson, Catherine Delicia, 25, 221, 229, 267, 270
Johnson, Hugh Walters Beaumont, 25
Johnson, Isabella, 25
Johnson, Victor George Ralph, 25
Joseph, Horace William Brindley, 91
Jowett, Benjamin, 7, 36-38, 41, 49, 72, 76, 84, 171, 242, 252, 256, 257, 271
Kant, Immanuel, 144, 146
Keble, John, 64, 128
Kegan Paul, Charles, 197, 199, 200, 203
Kelsall, John Edward, 236
Kensal Green (St Mary's Catholic cemetery), 13
Ketchum, Annie Chambers, 192
King, Edward, 144, 150, 186
Kingsley, Charles, 99
Knox-Little, William John, 132, 145, 150, 159, 186,

Landor, Walter Savage, 252
Landport, Hampshire (Winchester School Mission), 20, 190, 201, 204
Laud, William, 158
Leaflet, The, 32, 44, 50, 97, 103, 193, 223, 224, 265
Lee, Godfrey Bolles, 246
Lillie, Arthur, 77
Linklater, Robert, 190
Llewelyn Davies, John, 153
Loras College, Iowa, 16, 47, 49, 51
Loyola, Ignatius, 84
Lucian, 237, 263
Lucretius, 170, 268
Luke, Saint, 91
Lumby, John Rawson, 83
Macaulay, Thomas, 159
Mackmurdo, Arthur, 11
Maclagan, Edward Douglas, 70, 77
Mallock, W. H., 91
Manning, Henry Edward, 174
Mansel, Henry Longueville, 128
Marchant, John, 217
Marcus Aurelius, 263
Marillier, Henry Currie, 264, 267, 271, 272
Marlowe, Christopher, 162
Marson, Charles, 157, 165, 253
Maurice, Frederick Denison, 99, 128
Mazzini, Giuseppe, 109, 178
Medelssohn, Felix, 197
Mill, John Stuart, 71, 100, 154, 183, 237, 247
Milton, John, 124

Money-Kyrle, Rowland Tracy Asche, 221
Morris, Lewis, 79
Morris, William, 75, 78, 220, 224
Müller, Max, 88
Myers, F. W. H., 57, 58, 71, 83, 84, 109
New College, Oxford, 42, 44, 76, 91, 95, 113, 122, 132, 172, 203, 221, 223, 231, 242
Newman, John Henry, 28, 72, 115
Norman, William, 74
Norris, Francis Lushington, 201
Northcote, George Russell, 118, 136
Olcott, Henry Steel, 61-62, 86
Orange, Hugh William, 29, 229
Orred, Meta, 244
O'Shaughnessy, Arthur, 228, 240
Ovid, 106
Oxford, University of, 7, 9-11, 18, 20, 22, 25, 29, 33-34, 37-40, 49, 71, 72, 77, 88-89, 122, 142, 148, 153, 170-171, 175, 196, 224-225, 229-231, 233, 240, 243, 250-257, 273
Paley, William, 136
Pater, Walter, 8, 13, 225, 228, 238, 246
Pattison, Mark, 170
Paul, Saint, 57, 58, 71, 84, 92, 177, 183
Peacock, Thomas Love, 141-142
Pembroke Lodge, London, 33, 167, 215
Pittock, Murray, 10
Plarr, Victor, 14
Plato, 72-73, 91, 106, 139, 147, 256
Pound, Ezra, 11, 13-14, 188
Prisdang, Prince, 87
Psychical Research, Society for, 21

Putnam, Samuel P., 155
Pusey, Edward Bouverie, 76, 128, 150
Renan, Ernest, 84
Rhual, Wales, 33, 34, 155, 167, 168, 169, 208-209, 214, 226, 228
Richards, George Chatterton, 223, 224, 263, 265
Richardson, George ('Dick'), 23, 90, 93-94, 152, 166, 221, 267, 269, 272
Richardson, Sarah ('Mrs Dick'), 76, 78, 84, 153, 226, 259, 267, 269, 270, 271, 272, 273
Ridding, George, 58, 70, 73, 74, 75, 79, 83, 85, 93-94, 105, 115, 117, 119, 122, 252, 255, 258, 260, 262-263
Ridding, Lady Laura, 70, 74
Roberts, Charles Henry, 236
Roberts, Hugh Ainslie, 220
Robertson, James Craigie, 128
Roman Catholic Church, 11, 58, 60, 123, 129, 133, 135, 144, 147, 149, 150, 152
Roseliep, Raymond, 16, 49, 51-52
Rossetti, Christina, 102, 137, 156, 228, 247
Rossetti, Dante Gabriel, 140, 208, 214, 238
Rossetti, William Michael, 204, 224, 268
Rugby School, 30, 32, 97, 103, 113, 198-199, 223, 265
Runciman, James, 198
Ruskin, John, 78, 176, 204
Russell, Bertrand, 7, 8, 49, 51
Russell, Frances (formerly Lady John Russell), Countess Russell, 18, 23, 90, 167, 258-259
Russell, John (formerly Lord John Russell) first Earl Russell, 7, 19

Russell, John, Viscount Amberley, 92
Russell, Lady Mary Agatha, 188, 206-207, 220
Salvation Army, The, 70
Sand, George, 109
Santayana, George, 28, 38-39, 41
Sappho, 156, 162, 271
Sark, Isle of, 248
Scaliger, Joseph, 170
Schelling, Frederich Wilhelm Joseph, 146
Schopenhauer, Arthur, 104, 107, 146
Scott Holland, Henry, 149, 150, 151, 186
Scott, Lady Selina, 38
Scott, Mabel Edith, 38
Shakespeare, William, 66, 78, 79, 113, 161, 170, 191, 215
Shakespear, Dorothy, 188
Shakespear, Olivia, 188, 196, 212, 223, 251-252, 267
Shelley, Percy Bysshe, 17, 28, 30, 105, 115-116, 121, 123, 139, 141-142, 151, 154, 156, 161, 162, 169-171, 172, 173, 175, 178, 184, 185, 200, 203-205, 209, 210, 215, 222-224, 252, 255, 259, 272
Sinnett, A. P., 57, 62, 72, 73, 75, 86
Socrates, 73, 76, 192
Spencer, Edmund, 215
Spencer, Herbert, 161, 215
Spooner, William Archibald, 40, 42, 91, 221, 223, 252
Stanley, Arthur Penrhyn, 128
Stanley, Maude Alethea, 87
Stanton, George, 186
Stephen, James, 149
Stothard, George J., 224

Stothard, Thomas, 224
Swedenborg, Emanuel, 86, 88, 98, 108, 144-145, 237
Swinburne, Algernon Charles, 116, 119, 207, 226, 232, 238, 240, 248
Talbot, Bertram Chetwynd, 83-84
Taylor, Arnold Charles, 259
Temple, Frederick, 154
Tenby, Wales, 208-209, 211-213
Tertullian, 143-144
Theosophical Society, The, 61, 89
Thomson, James B. V., 121, 138, 210
Thorold, Anthony Wilson, 147, 157, 161, 165, 168, 178
Thucydides, 156
Thynne, John Alexander Roger ('Ion'), 231, 236, 240
Tennyson, Alfred, first Baron Tennyson, 78, 94, 107, 140, 170, 171, 188
Thomas à Kempis, 117, 135
Toynbee, Arnold, 154, 155, 157
Trusty Servant, The, 78-79, 83
Tylor, Edward R., 141
Unwin, Stanley, 8
Vidal, George Studley Sealy, 76, 242
Villon, François, 162
Voltaire, 162, 192
Walker, James, 236
Ward, Artemus, 135
Ward, Wilfred, 149
Waterfield, Reginald, 71
Welldon, James Edward Cowell, 265
Wells, Philip and George, 56
Wentworth, Thomas, first earl of Strafford, 159

Whitman, Walt, 31-32, 120, 125, 169-171, 173, 177, 180, 219, 226, 228, 238, 246, 250-252, 254-255, 257, 259, 260, 262-263, 265, 268
Wilberforce, Henry, 150
Wilde, James, first Baron Penzance, 173
Wilde, Oscar, 12
Winchester College, 9, 10, 18-21, 23-24, 27, 29, 34, 42, 50, 51, 55, 93-94, 110-111, 113, 149, 172, 199, 201, 202, 208-209, 212, 221, 228, 231, 240-242, 246-247, 249, 261, 263, 264-265, 267, 269, 271, 272
Wiseman, Nicolas, 150
Wordsworth, William, 106, 123-124, 216
Wright, Thomas, 13
Wykehamist, The, 20, 50, 78, 83, 85, 195-196, 199, 200, 201, 208, 226
Wykeham, William of, 172, 175
Yeats, W. B., 8, 13, 14, 28, 188
Y. M. C. A., 237

A PARTIAL LIST OF SNUGGLY BOOKS

ETHEL ARCHER *The Hieroglyph*
ETHEL ARCHER *Phantasy and Other Poems*
ETHEL ARCHER *The Whirlpool*
G. ALBERT AURIER *Elsewhere and Other Stories*
CHARLES BARBARA *My Lunatic Asylum*
S. HENRY BERTHOUD *Misanthropic Tales*
LÉON BLOY *The Tarantulas' Parlor and Other Unkind Tales*
ÉLÉMIR BOURGES *The Twilight of the Gods*
CYRIEL BUYSSE *The Aunts*
JAMES CHAMPAGNE *Harlem Smoke*
FÉLICIEN CHAMPSAUR *The Latin Orgy*
BRENDAN CONNELL *Unofficial History of Pi Wei*
BRENDAN CONNELL (editor)
   The Zaffre Book of Occult Fiction
BRENDAN CONNELL (editor)
   The Zinzolin Book of Occult Fiction
RAFAELA CONTRERAS *The Turquoise Ring and Other Stories*
ADOLFO COUVE *When I Think of My Missing Head*
RENÉ CREVEL *Are You All Crazy?*
QUENTIN S. CRISP *Aiaigasa*
LUCIE DELARUE-MARDRUS *The Last Siren and Other Stories*
LADY DILKE *The Outcast Spirit and Other Stories*
ÉDOUARD DUJARDIN *Hauntings*
BERIT ELLINGSEN *Now We Can See the Moon*
ERCKMANN-CHATRIAN *A Malediction*
ALPHONSE ESQUIROS *The Enchanted Castle*
ENRIQUE GÓMEZ CARRILLO *Sentimental Stories*
DELPHI FABRICE *Flowers of Ether*
DELPHI FABRICE *The Red Sorcerer*
DELPHI FABRICE *The Red Spider*
BENJAMIN GASTINEAU *The Reign of Satan*
EDMOND AND JULES DE GONCOURT *Manette Salomon*
REMY DE GOURMONT *From a Faraway Land*
REMY DE GOURMONT *Morose Vignettes*
GUIDO GOZZANO *Alcina and Other Stories*
GUSTAVE GUICHES *The Modesty of Sodom*

EDWARD HERON-ALLEN *The Complete Shorter Fiction*
EDWARD HERON-ALLEN *Three Ghost-Written Novels*
J.-K. HUYSMANS *The Crowds of Lourdes*
COLIN INSOLE *Valerie and Other Stories*
JUSTIN ISIS *Pleasant Tales II*
JULES JANIN *The Dead Donkey and the Guillotined Woman*
KLABUND *Spook*
GUSTAVE KAHN *The Mad King*
MARIE KRYSINSKA *The Path of Amour*
BERNARD LAZARE *The Mirror of Legends*
BERNARD LAZARE *The Torch-Bearers*
JULES LERMINA *Human Life*
MAURICE LEVEL *The Shadow*
JEAN LORRAIN *Errant Vice*
JEAN LORRAIN *Masks in the Tapestry*
GEORGES DE LYS *An Idyll in Sodom*
GEORGES DE LYS *Penthesilea*
ARTHUR MACHEN *Ornaments in Jade*
PAUL MARGUERITTE *Pantomimes and Other Surreal Tales*
CAMILLE MAUCLAIR *The Frail Soul and Other Stories*
CATULLE MENDÈS *Mephistophela*
ÉPHRAÏM MIKHAËL *Halyartes and Other Poems in Prose*
LUIS DE MIRANDA *Who Killed the Poet?*
OCTAVE MIRBEAU *The 628-E8*
OCTAVE MIRBEAU *The Death of Balzac*
CHARLES MORICE *Babels, Balloons and Innocent Eyes*
GABRIEL MOUREY *Monada*
DAMIAN MURPHY *Daughters of Apostasy*
KRISTINE ONG MUSLIM *Butterfly Dream*
OSSIT *Ilse*
CHARLES NODIER *Jean Sbogar and Other Stories*
CHARLES NODIER *Outlaws and Sorrows*
HERSH DOVID NOMBERG *A Cheerful Soul and Other Stories*
PHILOTHÉE O'NEDDY *The Enchanted Ring*
GEORGES DE PEYREBRUNE *A Decadent Woman*
HÉLÈNE PICARD *Sabbat*
JEAN PRINTEMPS *Whimsical Tales*
RACHILDE *The Princess of Darkness*

JEREMY REED *When a Girl Loves a Girl*
ADOLPHE RETTÉ *Misty Thule*
JEAN RICHEPIN *The Bull-Man and the Grasshopper*
FREDERICK ROLFE (**Baron Corvo**) *Amico di Sandro*
JASON ROLFE *An Archive of Human Nonsense*
ARNAUD RYKNER *The Last Train*
ROBERT SCHEFFER *Prince Narcissus and Other Stories*
ROBERT SCHEFFER *The Green Fly and Other Stories*
MARCEL SCHWOB *The Assassins and Other Stories*
MARCEL SCHWOB *Double Heart*
CHRISTIAN HEINRICH SPIESS *The Dwarf of Westerbourg*
BRIAN STABLEFORD (editor) *The Snuggly Satyricon*
BRIAN STABLEFORD (editor) *The Snuggly Satanicon*
BRIAN STABLEFORD *Spirits of the Vasty Deep*
COUNT ERIC STENBOCK *The Shadow of Death*
COUNT ERIC STENBOCK *Studies of Death*
MONTAGUE SUMMERS *The Bride of Christ and Other Fictions*
MONTAGUE SUMMERS *Six Ghost Stories*
ALICE TÉLOT *The Inn of Tears*
GILBERT-AUGUSTIN THIERRY *Reincarnation and Redemption*
DOUGLAS THOMPSON *The Fallen West*
TOADHOUSE *Gone Fishing with Samy Rosenstock*
TOADHOUSE *Living and Dying in a Mind Field*
TOADHOUSE *What Makes the Wave Break?*
LÉO TRÉZENIK *The Confession of a Madman*
LÉO TRÉZENIK *Decadent Prose Pieces*
RUGGERO VASARI *Raun*
ILARIE VORONCA *The Confession of a False Soul*
ILARIE VORONCA *The Key to Reality*
JANE DE LA VAUDÈRE *The Demi-Sexes and The Androgynes*
AUGUSTE VILLIERS DE L'ISLE-ADAM *Isis*
RENÉE VIVIEN *Lilith's Legacy*
RENÉE VIVIEN *A Woman Appeared to Me*
ILARIE VORONCA *The Confession of a False Soul*
ILARIE VORONCA *The Key to Reality*
TERESA WILMS MONTT *In the Stillness of Marble*
TERESA WILMS MONTT *Sentimental Doubts*
KAREL VAN DE WOESTIJNE *The Dying Peasant*

www.ingramcontent.com/pod-product-compliance
Lightning Source LLC
Chambersburg PA
CBHW060552080526
44585CB00013B/534